This inspiring book is a must read for all who care about advancing equity in education through literacy. Engaging and accessible, it includes a model for creating equitable learning environments that integrate three dimensions: quality instruction, opportunity, and representation. Rich perceptive vignettes showcase this evidence-informed model in action and practical ways forward are also offered. This wise and important book deserves to be widely shared to enable culturally responsive practice that enables all children to read proficiently and for pleasure.

Teresa Cremin, *Professor of Education (Literacy), The Open University, UK*

Adam's book provides an unapologetic testament to teaching reading in ways that honour children and families whilst reflecting their passions, beliefs, and literacy practices. The current literacy education crisis attacks what children bring to classrooms. While adopting packaged materials that supposedly serve all children is tempting, Adam refutes this approach's facility, reminding educators to leave space for exploration, creativity, and the important contributions of cultural and linguistic differences. This much-needed work challenges deficit perspectives and advocates for genuinely inclusive literacy environments.

Catherine Compton-Lily, *University of South Carolina, USA; John C. Hungerpiller Professor*

Having worked with Associate Professor Adam for many years, and seeing her work develop over time, I can categorically say this book is a must-read for policy makers and educators. We are what we see, or, in this case, read. Our children deserve to grow up seeing an accurate representation of themselves in the literature they consume and their teachings from a young age. This book will help pave the way for culturally responsive learning that empowers our children and young people now and into the future.

Jacqueline McGowan-Jones, *Commissioner for Children and Young People (Western Australia)*

Creating Equitable Literacy Learning Environments

This groundbreaking book introduces the Model for Equitable Literacy Learning Environments (MELLE), a comprehensive framework that integrates evidence-based instruction with culturally responsive pedagogy to create truly equitable learning environments for all children.

Despite decades of reading instruction reform, persistent achievement disparities remain between students from marginalised communities and their more privileged peers. Drawing on extensive international research across Australia, the United Kingdom, and the United States, the author examines how three key dimensions—quality instruction, opportunity to read, and authentic representation in reading materials—must work together within supportive cultural and community contexts. Interwoven with real-classroom examples, the text showcases how this framework can be applied to address persistent achievement gaps and promote inclusive education.

Moving beyond polarised literacy debates, this book is a must-read for educators seeking practical solutions to create equitable learning environments that empower learners from a range of backgrounds.

Helen Adam is an Associate Professor at Edith Cowan University, Western Australia and a 2022 Churchill Fellow. Her research focuses on culturally responsive and equitable literacy education. She has published extensively on anti-bias and equitable education through diverse literature in leading educational journals.

Creating Equitable Literacy Learning Environments

A Transformative Model

HELEN ADAM

LONDON AND NEW YORK

Designed cover image: The Model for Equitable Literacy Learning Environments (MELLE). Copyright © Helen Adam. Graphic design by Taylah Grey

First published 2026
by Routledge
4 Park Square, Milton Park, Abingdon, Oxon OX14 4RN

and by Routledge
605 Third Avenue, New York, NY 10158

Routledge is an imprint of the Taylor & Francis Group, an informa business

© 2026 Helen Adam

The right of Helen Adam to be identified as author of this work has been asserted in accordance with sections 77 and 78 of the Copyright, Designs and Patents Act 1988.

All rights reserved. No part of this book may be reprinted or reproduced or utilised in any form or by any electronic, mechanical, or other means, now known or hereafter invented, including photocopying and recording, or in any information storage or retrieval system, without permission in writing from the publishers.

Trademark notice: Product or corporate names may be trademarks or registered trademarks, and are used only for identification and explanation without intent to infringe.

British Library Cataloguing-in-Publication Data
A catalogue record for this book is available from the British Library

ISBN: 978-1-041-04402-4 (hbk)
ISBN: 978-1-041-04401-7 (pbk)
ISBN: 978-1-003-62821-7 (ebk)

DOI: 10.4324/9781003628217

Typeset in Dante and Avenir
by SPi Technologies India Pvt Ltd (Straive)

For Gloria, who inspired my career and, in doing so, changed my life and became my friend.

Contents

Foreword xi
Preface and Acknowledgments xiii

1 Introduction: The Reading Equity Dilemma 1

2 Theoretical Framework for Equitable Literacy Learning Environments 8

3 Quality Instruction: Rethinking 'Best Practice' 20

4 Opportunity Inequities in Access to Reading 41

5 Representation in Reading Materials 65

6 Disrupting Prejudice Through Children's Literature 86

7 The Model for Equitable Literacy Learning Environments 92

8 Culturally Responsive Literacy in Action: An Exemplar of Practice 118

9 Policy and Practice	130
10 Conclusion: Towards a New Paradigm in Reading Education	155
Appendix: Research Methodology	*162*
Index	*167*

Foreword
The Model for Equitable Literacy Learning Environments (MELLE): A Renaissance of Reading Instruction

When I was learning to read as a young child six decades ago, I was unaware that reading instruction was a contested topic. Though I now know about historic criticisms of the heavily behaviourist basal reading approaches used then, I also retrospectively realise that teachers in my racially segregated school had the presence of mind to adapt reading instruction based on what they knew about the children and our cultural backgrounds. Indeed, since laws prohibiting African diasporic people in the U.S. from reading and writing were repealed (and even before), Black teachers found ways to overcome Black-White racial literacy gaps and engaged children in night, pit, and later freedom schools. In these spaces, reading was purposeful and key to liberation. It was something that Black children *wanted* to do rather than a set of isolated skills for pronouncing words correctly. *Creating Equitable Literacy Learning Environments: A Transformative Model*, in many ways, represents a renaissance of culturally informed, child, family, and community-centred, common-sense literacy-rich reading instruction—not only for Black children, but for other children of colour, other minoritised groups, and White children as well.

Against a contentious backdrop of 'Reading Wars' about how best to teach young children to read, *Creating Equitable Literacy Learning Environments: A Transformative Model* offers a refreshing opportunity to start a movement which simultaneously—and comprehensively—focuses on the complexities involved in reading instruction. Recognising that the current debate about the most effective methods for teaching reading is shaped by evolving research and diverse perspectives within the field of literacy education, this book simultaneously offers both a critique of approaches which narrowly define the reading process and a framework for the way forward.

Dr. Helen Adam is deeply familiar with the existing knowledge bases and combines this with her wealth of experience. She understands that while some instructional approaches for reading have shown promise in certain contexts, research evidence remains mixed. Indeed, no single method has emerged as universally superior. Instead, a range of variables—including instructional context, language strategies employed and the specific literacy outcomes being measured (such as phonics skills or reading comprehension)—significantly influence research findings. As such, the search for effective literacy instruction demands a nuanced understanding that honours both the complexity of teaching and the diversity of learners.

Acknowledging this complexity, Dr. Adam introduces the *Model for Equitable Literacy Learning Environments* (MELLE) and advances a powerful lens for reimagining literacy instruction. The MELLE includes three interconnected dimensions; 1) quality instruction; 2) opportunity to read; and 3) representation. The MELLE positions literacy as dynamic, culturally rooted and multidimensional, encouraging educators to move beyond dichotomies and towards pedagogies that are rigorous, relevant and sustaining. Through this lens, literacy instruction is not only about what is taught, but also about whose knowledge, voices, and experiences are centred. In doing so, the MELLE reminds us that effective reading instruction must reflect the fullness of students' linguistic and cultural lives. The MELLE allows us to imagine a world where reading instruction is joyful and connected for children and teachers alike, rather than tedious and culturally irrelevant.

I embrace the MELLE framework because it allows me to imagine a time in my life when children enjoyed learning to read and teachers enjoyed teaching reading. The MELLE guides educators to embrace teachers' professional knowledge and judgement to figure out how to understand their students' needs, reading strategies, cultures and the complexities involved in reading instruction. This book is what is needed in this moment and time. To all readers, I say, "Read on!"

Gloria Swindler Boutte, PhD
Carolina Distinguished Professor, Early Childhood Education
University of South Carolina
AERA Social Justice in Education Award, 2025

Preface and Acknowledgments

I acknowledge that this book has been written on the unceded lands of the Whadjuk Noongar people, who have been educating children on Country for tens of thousands of years. As a White Australian researcher, I recognise my positioning within systems of privilege and hope this work contributes to amplifying the voices of First Nations people and others who are marginalised by political and educational systems, policies, and practices.

This book emerged from a decade-long journey of inquiry that began with a troubling observation: despite considerable advances in reading instruction research and policy, persistent disparities in literacy outcomes continue to disadvantage children from Indigenous, culturally and racially marginalised, and economically disadvantaged backgrounds.

The initial catalyst for this work was my doctoral research (2014–2019), which analysed over 2300 books and examined culturally responsive book-sharing practices in four Australian early childhood centres. I discovered significant disparities in both the quantity and quality of culturally responsive literacy practices between centres serving different socioeconomic communities—findings that prompted deeper questions about systemic factors creating inequitable literacy opportunities.

The transformative moment came through my Churchill Fellowship, which enabled eight weeks of intensive fieldwork in 2023 across the United States and the United Kingdom. I observed transformative pedagogies positioning children's cultural identities at the centre of literacy learning, witnessing remarkable shifts in engagement when students saw themselves authentically represented. Yet I also encountered devastating impacts of book censorship movements and persistent resource disparities leaving many schools serving marginalised communities inadequately supported. These experiences revealed that whilst specific manifestations of inequity varied across contexts, underlying challenges—and potential for transformation—were remarkably similar. Upon returning to Australia, I synthesised these insights with existing research to develop the Model for Equitable Literacy Learning Environments (MELLE). This framework integrates quality instruction, opportunity to read and representation within broader cultural, community and curricular contexts—recognising these not as competing priorities but as interconnected dimensions working in concert to create truly inclusive literacy education.

This book bridges the persistent divide between technical and critical approaches to literacy education, arguing that we need not choose between rigorous instruction and culturally responsive pedagogy. Written for policymakers, school leaders, educators, teacher educators and researchers, this book ultimately serves the children whose educational experiences depend on our collective commitment to creating more just and inclusive literacy learning environments.

I am deeply grateful to the Winston Churchill Memorial Trust of Australia, and to leadership and colleagues in the School of Education at Edith Cowan University, for providing the time, support and resources leading to the writing of this book. My appreciation extends to Doctoral Candidate Mikayla King; Principal Bill Boylan; ECU alumni teachers Keyan Robertson and Mitchell Paddick; and pre-service teachers Kate and Maya (pseudonyms), for generously sharing their vignettes of practice, alongside the many teachers and pre-service teachers who have participated in and contributed to my research, with particular thanks to Taylah Grey for graphic design.

This work has been enriched by my inspiring international network, including Gloria Boutte and colleagues, Mariana Souto-Manning and colleagues, Catherine Compton-Lilly, Ian Cushing, Teresa Cremin, Evelyn Arizpe, Navan Govender, Kyle Zimmer and Libby Jackson-Barrett. I am grateful for the insights gained through collaborations with the Children's Cooperative Book Center (Wisconsin), The Dollywood Foundation™ (Tennessee), the Centre for Literacy in Primary Education (London), First Book (Washington) and Children's Books Ireland.

My sincere thanks to Gloria Boutte, Teresa Cremin, Catherine Compton-Lilly and Jacqueline McGowan Jones for taking the time to read and endorse this book, and for their thoughtful reflections on its contributions to the field. I acknowledge the use of Claude Sonnet 4 (Anthropic) in exploring ideas, classifying literature, and refining language throughout the writing process.

Helen Adam CF
Edith Cowan University,
Western Australia

Introduction

The Reading Equity Dilemma

1

The Global Challenge of Equitable Education

Education systems worldwide continue to grapple with the profound challenge of ensuring equitable outcomes for all students. Despite decades of reform efforts, persistent achievement disparities between students from marginalised[1] communities—such as Indigenous populations, low-income families and many Culturally and Racially Minoritised[2] (CARM) groups—and their more privileged, mostly white, counterparts remain stubbornly wide. These disparities are particularly evident in literacy development, where reading proficiency serves as a critical gateway to academic success, lifelong learning, and socioeconomic mobility.

Countries including Australia, the United States and the United Kingdom face remarkably similar challenges in addressing these inequities. For nearly two decades, cognitive science research on how the brain learns to read has significantly influenced educational policies (Castles et al., 2018; Seidenberg, 2017; Tunmer & Hoover, 2019). This has led to mandated evidence-based practices in many educational institutions, including schools and Initial Teacher Education (ITE) (Australian Institute for Teaching and School Leadership, [AITSL] 2020a, 2020b, 2023). Yet, despite implementing these approaches, the same groups of students remain disproportionately represented in reading intervention and special education programmes (Cormier, 2023, 2024; Torres, 2024) and underrepresented in Gifted and Talented programmes. This ongoing disconnect suggests that while evidence-based reading instruction is important, it is insufficient alone to address equitable outcomes. The prevailing focus on cognitive science and "the brain" in education policy often overlooks the reality that these brains exist within children—complex, diverse individuals who arrive in classrooms with rich backgrounds, experiences and cultural knowledge that current reading instruction frequently fails to acknowledge or leverage. Thus, the emphasis on "evidence-based practice" in literacy policy presents a fundamental challenge for equity. While few would argue against using evidence, what constitutes "evidence" has been narrowly interpreted, often privileging methodologies from cognitive science while marginalising qualitative research and cultural perspectives. This restricted view has profound implications, as it frequently fails to account for the diverse cultural and linguistic resources that children bring to literacy learning. This tension between narrow and expansive understandings of evidence-based practice runs throughout current debates about reading instruction and will be explored in subsequent chapters.

Further complicating matters is the way in which discussions around reading instruction often position socioeconomic factors. While these factors are often cited as justification for explicit instruction methods, many socioeconomic factors—such as access to books, support for home literacy environments, and diverse family literacy practices—are frequently dismissed in policy discussions (Adam, 2023). As a result, the prevailing narrative often minimises these factors with phrases like "it's not about the postcode," undermining their significance in children's learning opportunities. Simultaneously, educational institutions are being urged to integrate culturally responsive practices to address inequities. However, for many educators, significant tensions and knowledge gaps exist about how culturally responsive approaches can be harmonised with evidence-based reading instruction. These approaches are often perceived as mutually exclusive and implemented in isolation from one another, creating a fractured educational landscape that serves neither purpose adequately.

This persistent achievement disparity is not merely an academic issue—it represents a fundamental matter of social justice. The separation of conversations about reading instruction from broader discussions of social equity has led to educational models that are not sufficiently responsive to the diverse needs and strengths of all students, despite often being promoted as founded on aims of social justice.

A Personal Journey and Global Perspective

In 2023, as a Churchill Fellowship recipient, I had the opportunity to spend eight weeks in the USA and the UK, meeting with leading scholars exploring ways in which children's literature can be a tool to challenge prejudice and discrimination. During this fellowship, I discovered that many of these scholars were frustrated with current approaches to teaching children—approaches that often exclude or marginalise the voices and experiences of diverse students, and indeed diverse academics, despite claims that many of these approaches are founded in social justice (Adam, 2023). In contrast, I also witnessed Initial Teacher Education (ITE) programmes and classrooms where diverse researchers were using their own lived experiences and understanding of marginalised communities to reshape reading instruction, transforming learning outcomes for children (Boutte, 2023; Braden et al., 2022; Erikson Institute, 2023; Wynter-Hoyte et al., 2022).

This book synthesises insights from the Churchill Fellowship, my own research over many years, and that of others into the importance of diverse books and culturally responsive practices. It offers educators, policymakers and community leaders a framework for addressing persistent inequities in reading and literacy instruction. While it critiques the limitations of current methods, its primary aim is to provide practical solutions for narrowing the achievement disparities that continue to disadvantage marginalised communities and providing truly inclusive and supportive education environments where all children feel they belong and know that their own lives and experiences are valued.

Towards a New Model for Equitable Literacy Instruction

The persistent achievement disparities and the limitations of current approaches point to the need for a new conceptual framework—one that holistically addresses reading and literacy instruction within its social, cultural and economic contexts. In Chapter 2, I present a comprehensive theoretical model for equitable literacy instruction built upon three key dimensions: quality instruction, opportunity to read, and representation, operating within environmental factors of culture, context, curriculum and community. This model is premised on the belief and evidence that effective reading instruction, and literacy instruction more broadly, cannot and should not be divorced from questions of equity and social justice. Evidence-based practices are incorporated within the model while the understanding of what constitutes "evidence" is expanded to include the lived experiences and perspectives of diverse communities. This model bridges the divide between cognitive science and culturally responsive pedagogy, offering a path towards more inclusive and effective literacy education.

Through engagement with this model, educators, policymakers and researchers are invited to move beyond polarised debates and consider a more nuanced understanding of how children learn to read in diverse contexts.

Scope and Focus of This Book

While the Model for Equitable Literacy Learning Environments (MELLE) presented in this book is applicable across all dimensions of literacy learning—including writing, speaking, viewing, and creating—this work primarily examines reading instruction and engagement. This focus on reading is intentional, as reading has been the site of particularly contentious debates about instruction and remains a critical gateway skill that enables access to other forms of literacy and learning.

Similarly, though equity in education encompasses multiple dimensions of diversity—including gender identity, sexual orientation, disability, socioeconomic status and their intersections—this book primarily examines cultural and linguistic diversity with particular attention to Indigenous and Culturally and Racially Minoritised (CARM) communities. This focus reflects both the emphases of my Churchill Fellowship research and the persistent inequities that have historically affected these communities in literacy education. The framework itself is designed with intersectionality in mind, recognising that children's identities are multifaceted and that different aspects of diversity interact in complex ways to shape educational experiences.

Conclusion: Towards a Vision for Equitable Literacy Instruction

This book offers a vision for equitable literacy instruction—one that moves beyond conversations of "what works" and instead focuses on the broader social, cultural and economic contexts in which students learn. It is time to rethink the environments and practices through which literacy, especially reading, is taught, ensuring that all children have access to high-quality, culturally responsive instruction and meaningful opportunities to engage with reading and literature that reflects their diverse experiences. The MELLE presented in the following chapters brings together three interconnected dimensions: quality instruction, opportunity and representation. Evidence-based practices are integrated with culturally responsive approaches within the model allowing for the creation of truly inclusive literacy environments where all students can develop as confident, engaged readers.

It is a collective responsibility to ensure that every child has access to diverse books, quality teaching practices and an education that recognises and celebrates their unique identities and backgrounds. By addressing the interconnected dimensions of instruction, opportunity and representation within supportive environmental factors, a more just and equitable educational future for all children can be created.

Notes

1 Marginalisation refers to the inequality certain individuals face in society due to power imbalances built into our systems.

> The issue of marginalisation then is inherently about unequal power relations that are built into our systems. It is about how, through these unequal power relations, our systems (including, but not limited to; law, politics, economics, and society itself) create hurdles that maintain the status quo. That status quo being, holding back and disadvantaging some groups, or leaving them "at the margins," (i.e. marginalised groups), while at the same time advantaging (i.e., privileging) dominant groups." Deo, S. (2023, 30/09/2024). Why we use the term "marginalised". https://www.dca.org.au/news/blog/why-we-use-the-term-marginalised.

2 Culturally and racially marginalised (CARM)—I use this term for the reasons given below taken from Diversity Council Australia.

> We use the term culturally and racially marginalised (CARM) to refer to people who cannot be racialised as white. This group includes people who are Black, Brown, Asian, or any other non-white group, who face marginalisation due to their race. The term "culturally" is added because it recognises that people may also face discrimination due to their culture or background. For example, a woman who is a Muslim migrant from South Sudan may face discrimination because of her race, religion and cultural background.

References

Adam, H. (2023). *Churchill Fellowship Report: To Enhance Expertise in Children's Books as Vehicles for Disrupting Prejudice and Discrimination*. https://www.churchilltrust.com.au/fellow/helen-adam-wa-2022/

Australian Institute for Teaching and School Leadership. (2020a). *Reading Instruction Evidence Guide Map*. https://www.aitsl.edu.au/docs/default-source/initial-teacher-edu.ation-resources/reading-instruction/reading-instruction-evidence-guide-map.pdf?sfvrsn=5665d73c_2

Australian Institute for Teaching and School Leadership. (2020b). *Sample Initial Teacher Education Program Outlines: Reading Instruction*. Australian Institute for Teaching and School Leadership Limited.

Australian Institute for Teaching and School Leadership. (2023). *Addendum: Accreditation of Initial Teacher Education Programs in Australia: Standards and Procedures*. https://www.aitsl.edu.au/docs/default-source/national-policy-framework/addendum-to-accreditation-standards-and-procedures.pdf

Boutte, G. (2023). *Educating African American Students: And How are the Children?* (2nd ed.). Routledge.

Braden, E., Boutte, G., Wynter-Hoyte, K., Long, S., Aitken, C., Collins, S., Frazier, J., Gamble, E., Hall, L., Hodge, S., McDonald, C., Merritt, A., Mosso-Taylor, S., Samuel, K., Stout, C., Tafel, J., Warren, T., & Witherspoon, J. (2022). Emancipating early childhood literacy curricula: Pro-black teaching in K-3 classrooms. *Journal of Early Childhood Literacy*, 22(4), 500–539.

Castles, A., Rastle, K., & Nation, K. (2018). Ending the reading wars: Reading acquisition from novice to expert. *Psychological Science in the Public Interest*, 19(1), 5–51. https://doi.org/10.1177/1529100618772271

Cormier, C. J. (2023). It's not easy being green: Addressing overrepresentation in special education through culturally responsive pedagogy. *Kappa Delta Pi Record*, 58, 10–15. https://doi.org/10.1080/00228958.2022.2132326

Cormier, C. J. (2024). Misidentification, misinformation, and miseducation: The experiences of minoritized students and representation in public schools across three societies around the globe. *PJE. Peabody Journal of Education*, 99(1), 1–3. https://doi.org/10.1080/0161956X.2024.2307792

Deo, S. (2023, September 30). *Why We Use the Term 'Marginalised'*. Diversity Council Australia. https://www.dca.org.au/news/blog/why-we-use-the-term-marginalised

Erikson Institute. (2023). *Master's of Early Childhood Education*. https://www.erikson.edu/academics/graduate-education/masters-degrees/early-childhood-education/

Seidenberg, M. S. (2017). *Language at the Speed of Sight: How We Read, Why So Many Can't, and What Can Be Done About It*. Basic Books.

Torres, G. (2024, August 14). NAPLAN results expose gap in education outcomes. *National Indigenous Times*. https://nit.com.au/14-08-2024/13110/naplan-results-expose-gap-in-education-outcomes

Tunmer, W. E. & Hoover, W. A., (2019). The cognitive foundations of learning to read: A framework for preventing and remediating reading difficulties. *Australian*

Journal of Learning Difficulties, 24(1), 75–93. https://doi.org/10.1080/19404158.2019.1614081

Wynter-Hoyte, K., Braden, E., Boutte, G., Long, S., & Muller, M. (2022). Identifying anti-Blackness and committing to Pro-Blackness in early literacy pedagogy and research: A guide for child care settings, schools, teacher preparation programs, and researchers. *Journal of Early Childhood Literacy, 22*(4), 565–591. https://doi.org/10.1177/14687984221135489

2 Theoretical Framework for Equitable Literacy Learning Environments

Introduction

The underlying premise of the Model for Equitable Literacy Learning Environments (MELLE) presented in this book is that technical expertise in literacy instruction must be coupled with critical consciousness and commitment to social justice. This book, and the design of the MELLE, address tensions that persist between these approaches, with proponents of evidence-based practice often critiquing critical literacy perspectives as ideologically driven rather than empirically grounded (Moats, 2020; Seidenberg, 2017) whilst critical theorists argue that evidence-based approaches to literacy on their own fail to address structural inequalities and cultural biases inherent in educational systems (Brock et al., 2023; Janks, 2010; Ladson-Billings, 2017; Wynter-Hoyte et al., 2022). This book argues both paradigms offer valuable insights when integrated thoughtfully. As argued by many critical scholars (Brock et al., 2023), effective literacy pedagogy requires both scientific understanding of reading development and critical awareness of how literacy practices are shaped by sociopolitical contexts, particularly for marginalised learners whose literacy experiences may be devalued by educational policy, mandated curriculum and dominant instructional models.

Therefore, I adopt a critical theoretical lens to examine how literacy instruction, opportunity and representation intersect with systems of power and privilege in education. Drawing on Critical Race Theory (Ladson-Billings, 2023) and critical pedagogy (Freire, 2000, 2014), this book is built upon a recognition that literacy education is not neutral but deeply embedded in social, political and cultural contexts. Simultaneously, it acknowledges the robust evidence base for effective reading instruction (Castles et al., 2018; Lonigan et al., 2009; Moats, 2020). The resulting MELLE can serve as a powerful support for education stakeholders to work towards equitable outcomes for all children.

Theoretical Foundations

The MELLE integrates critical perspectives with evidence-based instruction, recognising that both are essential for creating truly equitable literacy environments.

Critical Perspectives

This model is grounded in critical theory's examination of how power structures shape educational opportunities and outcomes. Through a Critical Race Theory lens (Ladson-Billings, 2023), literacy education can be understood as a site where racial inequities are both perpetuated and potentially transformed. Implicit in this conceptualisation is an examination of how literacy education "mediate/s messages that children receive about their cultures and roles in society" (Boutte et al., 2008, p. 943), revealing how seemingly neutral practices can reproduce social inequities through what is often termed the "hidden curriculum" (Apple, 2019; Jackson, 1968). Critical pedagogy (Freire, 2000) informs an understanding of literacy as a tool for empowerment and social transformation, while the concept of critical literacy (Morrell, 2017) emphasises reading not just as a technical skill but also as a means of analysing and challenging social inequities.

Thus, the foundation of the MELLE challenges restrictive interpretations of what constitutes 'evidence' in educational practice. Whilst 'evidence-based practice' has become prevalent in literacy education, its application often reflects a limited understanding that privileges particular research methodologies—typically randomised controlled trials and large-scale quantitative studies—over other forms of knowledge generation.

The MELLE adopts a more expansive conception that acknowledges multiple ways of knowing and diverse research traditions, creating space for instructional approaches that are simultaneously rigorous and responsive to diverse cultural contexts—a tension that will be explored more fully in Chapter 3.

Evidence-Based Instruction

The MELLE is designed with both a critical perspective and an integration of prevailing evidence on effective reading instruction. Cognitive science studies have established strong evidence for systematic, explicit teaching approaches (often termed 'evidence-based' and/or the 'Science of Reading') (Castles et al., 2018; Ehri, 2020; Lonigan et al., 2009), particularly for the constrained skills of reading such as phonics. However, this book argues that such instruction must be implemented within a broader commitment to equity and social justice that focuses on more than reading proficiency and test results. This integration addresses what Paris and Alim identify as a false dichotomy between rigorous instruction and cultural responsiveness (2014, 2017). Evidence-based practices in phonics instruction, vocabulary development and comprehension strategies can and must be delivered through culturally sustaining pedagogies.

Therefore, in the MELLE, literacy equity is conceptualised through both distributional and recognitive justice lenses (Fraser, 2013; Keddie, 2012). This means attending not only to access to resources and quality instruction but also to the rich linguistic and cultural resources that children from all backgrounds bring to their literacy, as well as to whose knowledge is valued, whose stories are told, and whose voices are heard in literacy education (Figure 2.1).

Presenting the Model for Equitable Literacy Learning Environment (MELLE)

The MELLE synthesises these theoretical perspectives into a comprehensive model for creating equitable literacy environments. This model comprises three core dimensions—quality instruction, opportunity to read and representation—all situated within contextual factors of culture, community, context and curriculum. The following chapters of this book will present each key dimension along with evidence of why each matters, and can be harnessed, to create equitable literacy environment learning to equitable outcomes.

Theoretical Framework for Equitable Literacy Learning Environments 11

Figure 2.1 The model for equitable literacy learning environments.

Box 2.1 Key Terminology

Key Terminology: Understanding Cultural Approaches to Pedagogy

Throughout this book, several related terms describe approaches that centre cultural knowledge in education. While sometimes used interchangeably in broader discourse, they represent an evolving theoretical tradition with important distinctions:

Culturally Responsive Pedagogy (CRP): Developed by Gloria Ladson-Billings (1995, 2014) and further advanced by Geneva Gay (2010, 2018), CRP emphasises teaching practices that respond to and incorporate students' cultural knowledge, prior experiences and performance styles. It focuses on using "cultural knowledge, prior experiences, frames of reference, and performance styles of ethnically diverse students to make learning more relevant and effective" (Gay, 2010, p. 31).

Culturally Relevant Teaching (CRT): Often used synonymously with CRP, this term was initially developed by Ladson-Billings (1995) with specific emphasis on three pillars: academic success, cultural competence and sociopolitical consciousness. Culturally relevant teaching particularly emphasises developing students' critical consciousness about societal inequities.

Culturally Sustaining Pedagogy (CSP): Building upon the foundations of CRP and CRT, Django Paris and H. Samy Alim (2014, 2017) introduced this term to emphasise not just responding to culture but actively sustaining and fostering linguistic, literate, and cultural pluralism. CSP "seeks to perpetuate and foster—to sustain—linguistic, literate, and cultural pluralism as part of schooling for positive social transformation" (2017, p. 1).

In the MELLE framework, I acknowledge the important theoretical developments across these approaches. While I primarily use "culturally responsive pedagogy" as an umbrella term throughout this book, the model incorporates elements from all three perspectives, recognising their complementary contributions to equitable literacy education.

Framework Scope and Contextual Considerations

The MELLE framework emerges from research conducted primarily within English-speaking educational contexts, with particular emphasis on Australian, American and British systems. Whilst the theoretical foundations and core dimensions of quality instruction, opportunity and representation have broad applicability, implementation requires careful attention to local cultural knowledge systems, community priorities and existing educational structures. This framework represents an initial theorisation that prioritises depth of understanding over breadth of application, offering a flexible structure for examining how literacy equity manifests within specific contexts rather than providing universal prescriptions. The qualitative methodological approach, detailed in Appendix 1, emphasises rich contextual insights that call for thoughtful adaptation honouring both the core principles of equity and the unique characteristics of each learning community—reflecting the underlying principles of the MELLE in ensuring a fundamental commitment to recognising diverse ways of knowing and being.

Core Dimensions Through a Critical Lens

Quality Instruction

Quality instruction forms the first dimension of the model, encompassing both the technical aspects of effective reading instruction and the critical dimensions of culturally responsive and sustaining pedagogy.

Quality instruction in this model means:

- Incorporating evidence-based practices for teaching foundational skills

Doing so while:

- Recognising and valuing the linguistic resources students bring to literacy learning
- Challenging deficit perspectives that conceptualise marginalised children's language and knowledge as problematic
- Creating instructional contexts where diverse learners see their identities affirmed

While acknowledging the importance of systematic instruction in foundational skills, Chapter 3 will examine how instructional approaches can either challenge or reinforce existing power structures. Rather than focusing on 'fixing' children from marginalised communities, quality instruction empowers students by recognising the value of their diverse knowledge, experiences, literacy practices and languages.

Opportunity to Read

The second represents the critical issue of access—specifically, the disparities in opportunities to read that exist between children from differing socioeconomic backgrounds and cultural contexts.

Opportunity in this model encompasses:

- Physical access to diverse, high-quality books
- Time dedicated to reading during the school day
- Support for developing reading identities and reading for pleasure
- Access to knowledgeable educators and librarians
- Home–school connections that value diverse literacy practices

Chapter 4 will confront the paradox in some evidence-based reading programmes and practices that emphasise skills acquisition but often fail to provide students with opportunities to engage in meaningful, enjoyable and critical reading experiences where they can apply these skills. For children from low socioeconomic backgrounds, who may have limited access to books at home or in their communities, ensuring ample opportunity to read at school becomes particularly crucial.

Thus, the MELLE framework illustrates that meaningful reading opportunity extends beyond mere access to books to include supportive contexts for engagement. This includes well-resourced libraries with qualified librarians, dedicated time for independent reading, and pedagogical approaches that foster intrinsic motivation and reading identity.

Representation

The third-dimension addresses representation in literacy materials, moving beyond superficial notions of diversity to examine the quality, authenticity and critical potential of texts.

Effective representation in this model means:

- Authentic portrayal of diverse identities, experiences and perspectives in multiple texts
- Critical examination of how power and privilege operate in texts
- Challenging dominant narratives and stereotypes
- Affirming the identities and experiences of marginalised students

Chapter 5 explores the rationale for this dimension, building on Bishop's (1990) mirrors, windows and sliding glass doors concept. What students read profoundly impacts how they see themselves and others. The lack of diverse representation can both alienate marginalised students and reinforce notions of superiority for children from dominant cultural backgrounds. This dimension extends beyond token inclusion to examine whose stories are told, by whom and to what end. Research demonstrates that when students encounter texts reflecting their identities, they show increased engagement, comprehension and positive reading attitudes. For students from dominant backgrounds, diverse texts provide essential 'windows' into others' experiences, fostering empathy. Thus, representation serves both academic and social justice purposes, supporting literacy development while disrupting harmful stereotypes and prejudices.

Sociocultural Factors

The three core dimensions of the model operate within a broader context shaped by four sociocultural factors: culture, community, context and curriculum.

Culture/s: School and classroom culture plays a critical role in shaping students' attitudes towards reading and writing. A culture that values diversity encourages risk-taking and fosters collaboration, creating conditions where all students can thrive as readers and writers. This factor examines how cultural norms and expectations either support or hinder equitable literacy development.

Community: The community factor recognises that literacy learning extends beyond the classroom walls. It encompasses partnerships with families and engagement with the broader community context. This factor emphasises the importance of recognising and building upon the 'funds of knowledge' (Moll et al., 1992) that exist within students' communities, challenging deficit views of marginalised communities.

Context: The context factor acknowledges the specific conditions in which literacy instruction occurs, including geographic location, available resources and the sociopolitical environment. This factor recognises that equity does not mean identical approaches for all students but rather responsive instruction that addresses specific needs and circumstances of each learning community.

Curriculum: The curriculum factor examines both official and enacted curriculum, including required standards, approved materials and assessment practices. It recognises that curriculum is never neutral but reflects particular values, perspectives and power relationships. This factor encourages critical examination of curriculum to identify whose knowledge is centred and whose experiences are marginalised.

Conclusion—Implementation Through a Critical Praxis

Implementing the MELLE necessitates what Freire (2000) terms "critical praxis"—the deliberate integration of reflection and action to transform inequitable systems. This approach demands coordinated effort across multiple domains of educational practice, recognising that systemic change requires both theoretical understanding and practical engagement with existing power structures.

The MELLE framework emerges from a rigorous research trajectory spanning a decade, combining multiple methodologies and diverse data sources. This foundation includes doctoral research examining culturally responsive literacy practices, international fieldwork through the Churchill Fellowship, and collaborative inquiry cycles with educators across varied contexts. Readers seeking deeper understanding of these methodological underpinnings are directed to Appendix 1, which details the comprehensive research process informing this model.

Creating truly equitable literacy environments requires sophisticated integration of multiple perspectives that transcends traditional educational dichotomies. At its core, this work demands the thoughtful synthesis of critical theoretical frameworks with evidence-based instructional approaches, ensuring that technical excellence in literacy instruction not only coexists with but actively reinforces transformative social justice goals. This integration challenges the false choice between rigorous instruction and cultural responsiveness that has characterised much educational discourse. Within the MELLE, excellence and equity in literacy education are conceptualised as inextricably linked rather than competing priorities. Strong literacy instruction serves as an essential foundation for social transformation and personal empowerment, while careful attention to equity ensures that all students—regardless of background or circumstance—benefit meaningfully from high-quality instruction and equitable opportunity. This reciprocal relationship creates the conditions for both academic achievement and social transformation.

The chapters that follow will explore each dimension of the model in greater depth, offering practical strategies and authentic exemplars of successful implementation across diverse educational contexts. While creating equitable literacy environments undoubtedly presents complex challenges, these examples will demonstrate that meaningful change is both necessary and achievable when educators commit to addressing quality instruction, opportunity to read and representation within supportive environmental contexts. This comprehensive approach creates literacy spaces where all students feel valued, supported and empowered to succeed not merely as readers and writers but also as active participants in a more just society. This represents not simply an educational imperative but a moral commitment to creating a more equitable world through literacy's transformative potential.

References

Apple, M. W. (2019). *Ideology and Curriculum* (4th ed.). Routledge.

Bishop, R. S. (1990). Mirrors, windows and sliding glass doors. *Perspectives; Choosing and Using Books for the Classroom*, 6(3), ix–xi.

Boutte, G. S., Hopkins, R., & Waklatsi, T. (2008). Perspectives, voices, and worldviews in frequently read children's books. *Early Education and Development*, 19(6), 941–962. https://doi.org/10.1080/10409280802206643

Brock, C. H., Exley, B., & Rigney, L.-I. (2023). *International Perspectives on Literacies, Diversities, and Opportunities for Learning: Critical Conversations*. Routledge. https://doi.org/10.4324/9781003179061

Castles, A., Rastle, K., & Nation, K. (2018). Ending the reading wars: Reading acquisition from novice to expert. *Psychological Science in the Public Interest*, 19(1), 5–51. https://doi.org/10.1177/1529100618772271

Ehri, L. C. (2020). The science of learning to read words: A case for systematic phonics instruction. *Reading Research Quarterly*, 55(S1), S45–S60. https://doi.org/10.1002/rrq.334

Fraser, N. (2013). *Scales of Justice: Reimagining Political Space in a Globalizing World*. Wiley.

Freire, P. (2000). *Pedagogy of the Oppressed* (30th anniversary ed.). Continuum.

Freire, P. (2014). *Pedagogy of Hope*. Bloomsbury Academic.

Gay, G. (2010). *Culturally Responsive Teaching* (2nd ed.). Teachers College Press.

Gay, G. (2018). *Culturally Responsive Teaching: Theory, Research, and Practice* (3rd ed.). Teachers College Press.

Jackson, P. W. (1968). *Life in Classrooms*. Teachers College Press.

Janks, H. (2010). *Literacy and Power*. Routledge. https://doi.org/10.4324/9780203869956

Keddie, A. (2012). Schooling and social Justice through the lenses of Nancy Fraser. *Critical Studies in Education*, *53*(3), 263–279. https://doi.org/10.1080/17508487.2012.709185

Ladson-Billings, G. (1995). Toward a theory of culturally relevant pedagogy. *American Educational Research Journal*, *32*(3), 465–491.

Ladson-Billings, G. (2014). Culturally relevant pedagogy 2.0: a.k.a. the remix. *Harvard Educational Review*, *84*(1), 74–84.

Ladson-Billings G. (2017). The (r)evolution will not be standardized: Teacher education, hip hop pedagogy, and culturally relevant pedagogy 2.0. In D. Paris, & H. S. Alim (Eds.), *Culturally Sustaining Pedagogies: Teaching and Learning for Justice in a Changing World* (pp. 141–156). Teachers College Press.

Ladson-Billings, G. (2023). Just what is Critical Race Theory and what's it oing in a nice field like education? In E. Taylor, D. Gillborn, & G. Ladson-Billings (Eds.), *Foundations of Critical Race Theory in Education* (3rd ed.). Routledge. https://doi.org/10.4324/b23210

Lonigan, C. J., Shanahan, T., & National Institute for Literacy (2009). *Developing Early Literacy: Report of the National Early Literacy Panel. Executive Summary. A Scientific Synthesis of Early Literacy Development and Implications for Intervention*. National Institute for Literacy.

Moats, L. C. (2020). Teaching reading "Is" rocket science: What expert teachers of reading should know and be able to do. *American Educator*, *44*(2), 4–9.

Moll, L. C., Amanti, C., Neff, D., & Gonzalez, N. (1992). Funds of knowledge for teaching: Using a qualitative qpproach to connect homes and classrooms. *Theory into Practice*, *31*(2), 132–141.

Morrell, E. (2017). Toward equity and diversity in literacy research, policy, and practice: A critical, global approach. *Journal of Literacy Research*, *49*(3), 454–463. https://doi.org/10.1177/1086296X17720963

Paris, D., & Alim, H. S. (2014). What are we weeking to sustain through culturally sustaining pedagogy? A loving critique forward. *Harvard Educational Review*, *84*(1), 85–100. https://doi.org/10.17763/haer.84.1.982l873k2ht16m77

Paris, D., & Alim, H. S. (2017). *Culturally Sustaining Pedagogies: Teaching and Learning for Justice in a Changing World*. Teachers College Press.

Seidenberg, M. S. (2017). *Language at the Speed of Sight: How We Read, Why so Many Can't, and What Can Be Done About It*. Basic Books.

Wynter-Hoyte, K., Braden, E., Boutte, G., Long, S., & Muller, M. (2022). Identifying anti-Blackness and committing to pro-Blackness in early literacy pedagogy and research: A guide for child care settings, schools, teacher preparation programs, and researchers. *Journal of Early Childhood Literacy*, *22*(4), 565–591. https://doi.org/10.1177/14687984221135489

Quality Instruction

Rethinking 'Best Practice'

Introduction—The *What* and *How* of Reading Instruction Too Often Obscures the *Who* and *Why*

For decades, educational discourse surrounding children's literacy acquisition has centred on two fundamental questions: what skills children need to become successful readers and how these skills should be taught. Within these discussions, literacy—particularly reading—is frequently reduced to a discrete set of skills, often leading to deficit-based narratives when considering student diversity. This is especially evident in discussions about children from low socioeconomic, Indigenous, Culturally and Racially Marginalised (CARM) and English as an Additional Language/Dialect (EAL/D) backgrounds.

This chapter examines how the narrow focus on skills and instruction has intensified standardised approaches and assessment regimes, bolstered by claims that identical evidence-based methods can ensure success for all children. While these approaches rest on substantial research, the evidence base warrants critical examination. Much of the foundational research informing current reading instruction policies emerged from studies either focusing on children with learning difficulties or special educational needs (Seidenberg, 2024) or drawing from samples overrepresenting white middle-class populations (Comber & Woods, 2018; Souto-Manning et al., 2018; Washington & Seidenberg, 2021). As Gutiérrez and Larson (1994) observed three decades ago, such research frequently abstracts reading from its sociocultural contexts, treating literacy as a neutral technical skill rather than a socially situated practice. Over time, these influences have evolved into a broadly accepted assumption that standardised approaches will be optimal for all learners—a simplified 'one-size-fits-all' approach that key pioneer of the Science of Reading, Seidenberg, has recently questioned (2024). Importantly, this standardisation exists alongside substantial research challenging its underlying premises.

The chapter will examine the evolution of evidence-based practice in reading instruction, highlighting the valuable contribution while identifying limitations for diverse learners. It explores how difference is often positioned within deficit frames, particularly regarding linguistic diversity. Moving beyond critique, it presents asset-based approaches that recognise the diverse knowledge all children bring to literacy learning. Finally, it discusses integrative approaches that successfully combine explicit instruction with culturally responsive pedagogies, demonstrating how quality instruction forms a critical dimension of the Model for Equitable Literacy Learning Environments (MELLE) presented in this book.

Theoretical Foundations of Reading

The Four Resources Model and Its Place in Reading Development Theory

Literacy and reading instruction have evolved through multiple theoretical traditions, each contributing valuable insights into how humans acquire and develop reading skills. The Four Resources Model (Freebody & Luke, 1990), developed in Australia, provided a foundational framework that informs the MELLE presented in this book. Unlike approaches focused primarily on cognitive processes, this model conceptualises effective reading through four interconnected roles or families of practices:

1. The code breaker (decoding text)
2. The text participant (comprehending meaning)
3. The text user (understanding functional aspects of texts)
4. The text analyst (critically analysing texts)

This framework explicitly acknowledges the sociocultural dimensions of literacy, positioning reading as both a technical skill and a social practice embedded in specific cultural contexts. The model was later expanded (Luke

& Freebody, 1999) to emphasise that these are not merely skills but social practices that readers must develop to participate fully in literate societies.

The Evolution of Reading Theory: From Simple Models to Complex Frameworks

Since the early 2000s, the landscape of reading instruction has undergone a profound transformation, spearheaded by landmark inquiries conducted in three major English-speaking nations. The United States' National Reading Panel Report (2000) identified five essential components: phonemic awareness, phonics, fluency, vocabulary and comprehension. These findings were subsequently reinforced by the Australian National Inquiry into the Teaching of Literacy (2005) and the UK's Independent Review of the Teaching of Early Reading (Rose, 2006). In 2014, Australian researcher Deslea Konza proposed expanding these to the 'Big Six' by explicitly incorporating oral language development (2014), highlighting that oral language competency forms the bedrock upon which other reading skills are built.

Theoretical understanding of reading development has been substantially deepened by advances in cognitive science. Stanislas Dehaene's (2009) work on how brains learn to read opened new avenues for understanding how the human brain adapts to process written language. This foundation has been built upon by numerous scholars: Castles et al. (2018) illuminated the cognitive mechanisms underlying successful reading acquisition; Ehri (2020, 2023) advanced understanding of word learning and orthographic mapping; and Seidenberg (2017) bridged the gap between cognitive science and educational practice. Thus, cognitive science has emerged as particularly influential through evidence-based insights into phonological awareness, systematic phonics instruction and the cognitive processes underlying reading.

Theoretical models have also evolved to conceptualise the interconnected nature of reading skills. The Simple View of Reading, proposed by Gough and Tunmer (1986), provided a foundational framework by positing reading comprehension as the product of decoding ability and language comprehension. Scarborough's Reading Rope model offered a more detailed visualisation of various skills 'woven' together in skilled reading, while Hoover and Tunmer's Cognitive Foundations Framework (2020) further elaborated on the underlying cognitive processes that support reading development.

Significantly, many developers of these influential models also acknowledge their limitations. Tunmer and Hoover (2019) recognised that the Cognitive

Foundations Framework does not fully capture the complexity of reading development across diverse cultural contexts:

> The (Cognitive Foundations) Framework is concerned with the cognitive foundations underlying learning to read. As such, it does not deal with other important factors that may indirectly impact reading acquisition. These include psychological factors such as motivation to learn to read, interest in reading, and self-efficacy, and ecological factors such as richness of the home literacy environment and quality of classroom literacy instruction.
>
> (pp. 76–77)

In response to these recognised limitations, Duke and Cartwright (2021) proposed the Active View of Reading, which explicitly incorporates elements overlooked in previous models, including self-regulation, motivation and sociocultural context. This more comprehensive model acknowledges that successful reading involves not just cognitive skills but also reader identity, cultural knowledge and strategic thinking (Figure 3.1).

Duke and Cartwright (2021) note the growing complexity of reading theories, referencing Seidenberg et al.'s (2020) observation that these theories have become "more complex and less intuitive as the field has progressed" (p. S119). They argue that while the Simple View of Reading has become dominant in the current 'Science of Reading' movement, educators would benefit from exposure to more comprehensive models that better reflect the multifaceted nature of reading development and can more effectively accommodate diverse learners' needs and experiences.

The Four Resources Model in the MELLE Framework

Despite the evolution of various reading models over the past decades, the Four Resources Model (Freebody & Luke, 1990) remains particularly valuable to the MELLE framework for several compelling reasons. First, unlike models focused primarily on cognitive processes, it explicitly acknowledges reading as both a technical skill and a social practice—directly aligning with the MELLE's illustration that literacy development occurs within specific cultural and social contexts. Second, its inclusion of the text analyst role centralises critical literacy—a dimension often minimised in cognitive models but essential for equitable literacy education that empowers all learners. Third, the model's conceptualisation of reading roles as social

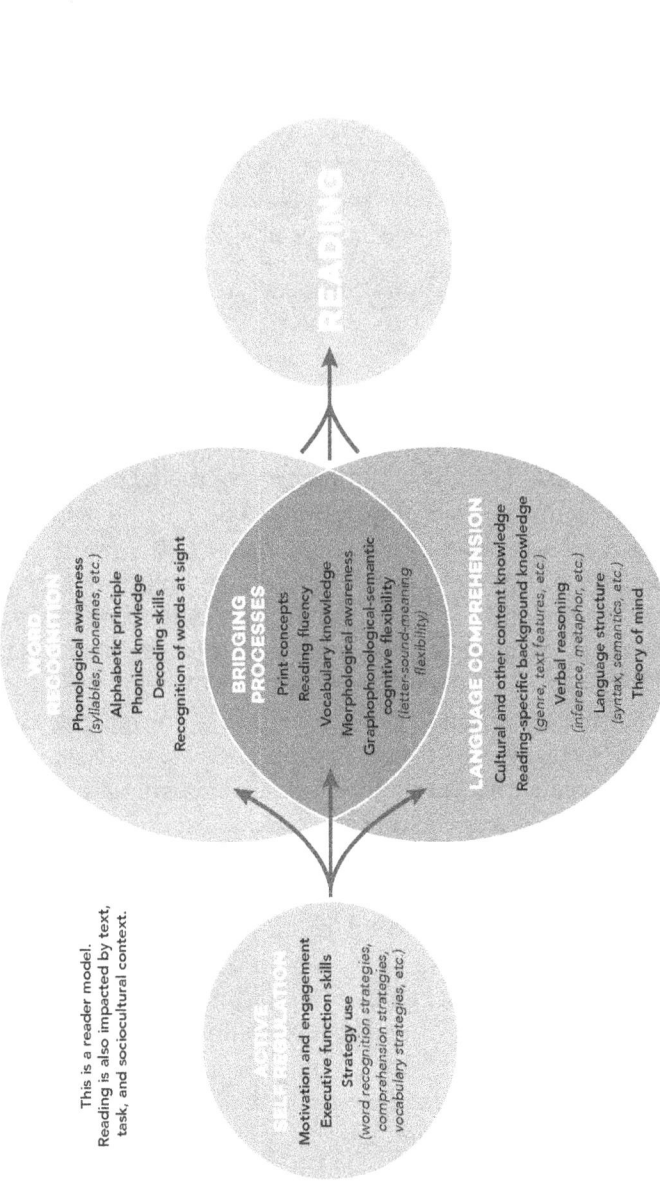

Figure 3.1 The active view of reading. (Duke & Cartwright, 2021).
Reprinted from "The science of reading progresses: Communicating advances beyond the Simple View of Reading," by N. K. Duke and K. B. Cartwright, 2021, Reading Research Quarterly, 56(S1), S25–S44. Copyright 2021 Authors. Reprinted with permission.

Author's Note: Several wordings in this model are adapted from Scarborough (2001).

practices rather than merely individual competencies resonates with the MELLE's emphasis on how literacy practices are shaped by opportunity and representation.

Notably, while the Four Resources Model (Freebody & Luke, 1990) predates the major reading inquiries, it demonstrates remarkable compatibility with their findings. The model's code breaker role aligns directly with the National Reading Panel's emphasis on phonemic awareness, phonics and decoding skills. Its text participant role encompasses the fluency, vocabulary and comprehension components highlighted in all three inquiries. The text user and text analyst roles extend beyond these inquiries to address the application and critical evaluation of texts—dimensions that have gained increasing recognition as essential to comprehensive literacy development. This harmony between the Four Resources Model and subsequent reading research underscores its enduring relevance and explanatory power.

As Duke and Cartwright (2021) note, reading theories have become "more complex and less intuitive as the field has progressed," yet the Four Resources Model maintains its accessibility and practical utility precisely because it offers a comprehensible, yet comprehensive framework that accommodates both cognitive and sociocultural dimensions of reading. Unlike some newer, highly technical models that may be difficult for educators to translate into practice, the Four Resources Model provides clear guidance for instruction while still addressing the full complexity of reading development.

Thus, the Four Resources Model (Freebody & Luke, 1990) provides a comprehensive framework that accommodates both the technical aspects of reading instruction emphasised by cognitive science and the sociocultural dimensions highlighted by critical literacy perspectives. This synergy is central to the MELLE framework, which similarly seeks to integrate quality instruction (addressing code-breaking and comprehension) with opportunity and representation (supporting engagement as text users and text analysts). When children develop capabilities across all four resources—breaking the code, making meaning, using texts for specific purposes and critically analysing texts—they become fully empowered literacy learners.

The evolution of models and approaches to teaching reading suggests that progress in understanding reading development requires drawing from multiple research traditions rather than privileging any single perspective. Thus, I argue, it is past time to move beyond sides to a more unified approach that acknowledges the complexities, the developmental sequences and the diverse needs of different populations of students. A more integrated understanding can create space for instructional approaches that honour both the cognitive and sociocultural dimensions of learning to read.

Rethinking 'Evidence-Based' Practice

Both the Four Resources Model and cognitive science research have contributed valuable insights to reading instruction. However, the term 'evidence-based practice' pervades educational discourse, yet is often narrowly interpreted. In reading instruction, it has frequently been restricted to findings from cognitive science and experimental studies focusing on constrained skills like phonemic awareness and phonics. While valuable, such evidence represents only one segment of the broader research spectrum necessary for comprehensive reading instruction. As such, Comber and Woods (2018) advocate for an inclusive understanding of evidence that extends beyond randomised controlled trials and quantitative studies to encompass qualitative research, classroom case studies and documented practitioner knowledge. This expanded view acknowledges that different educational questions require diverse methodological approaches. For example, while experimental studies may effectively identify which phonics approaches yield the strongest short-term decoding outcomes, ethnographic research better illuminates how classroom contexts and cultural factors influence the implementation and effectiveness of those approaches. Similarly, participatory research with diverse communities can provide essential insights into how reading practices are experienced by different groups of learners—insights that cannot be captured through standardised assessments alone. Seidenberg himself, in his recent analysis of the Science of Reading movement, argues for "a better mix of different kinds of learning experiences" (2024, p. 9), including both explicit instruction and implicit learning opportunities. He cautions that "heavy reliance on explicit instruction…is not optimal for typically developing children" (2024, p. 12) and expresses concern that "the SoR seems to be applying the same approach to all" (2024, p.12). When a leading proponent of evidence-based instruction raises such concerns, it underscores the importance of a more nuanced approach to reading instruction.

Washington and Seidenberg (2021) extend this understanding through their work on African American English (AAE) and literacy development emphasising that "speaking AAE is not inherently an obstacle to becoming a reader, but it becomes one when children's specific needs are not recognised or addressed" (p. 30). Their research shows that educators without language variation awareness may misinterpret linguistic differences as learning deficits, leading to inappropriate responses. They further critique how standardised assessments systematically disadvantage speakers of non-dominant language varieties:

> Psychometrically, many standardized instruments have been found to lack sensitivity when used with children from low-income families and with speakers of language varieties, making it more likely that their strengths will be overlooked. Clinically, studies focused on language differences versus language disorders have highlighted significant overlap between the linguistic features of AAE and features of language impairment, making it more likely that AAE speakers will be misdiagnosed and identified as language impaired when no impairment exists.
>
> (p. 30)

The Australian Council of TESOL (Teaching English to Speakers of Other Languages) Associations makes similar warnings regarding mandated requirements for ITE Education in Australia regarding approaches to phonics teaching:

> The recommendations for mandated phonics instruction in early reading assume that all students have age-appropriate fluency in spoken English and ignore the significance of oral language and first language literacy skills in learning literacy and the role of cultural and content knowledge in gaining meaning from texts. They do not address the long-term English reading comprehension needs of EAL/D learners across the years and key transitions of schooling. These mono-lingual assumptions are liable to mis-assess EAL/D students' learning needs as stemming from some kind of disability.
>
> (ACTA/ATESOL, 2022, p. 11)

These critiques are powerfully supported by recent empirical evidence. Research by Dobrescu et al. (2022), explored further in Chapter 7, found that simply adapting standardised NAPLAN test questions to include contextually familiar references for Aboriginal and rural Australian students reduced achievement gaps by up to 50%. This suggests that what is often measured as 'reading difficulties' may often reflect assessment bias rather than actual skill deficits. Together, these findings underscore the need for evidence-based practice to incorporate insights from sociolinguistic research alongside cognitive science, and to develop assessment approaches that recognise and value linguistic diversity rather than penalising it.

Narrow interpretations of evidence-based practice have delegitimised pedagogical approaches rooted in sociocultural and critical traditions, despite evidence of their effectiveness for diverse learners (López, 2016; Martinez, 2018). Truly comprehensive evidence-based reading instruction should acknowledge that no single research tradition holds all answers—multiple perspectives are essential for addressing the complex challenges of literacy education in diverse societies (Allington, 2013; Comber, 2015). This recognition necessitates an examination of how difference is often framed as deficit in educational contexts.

Deficit Framing and the Privileging of White Middle-Class Literacy Practices

For decades, diverse researchers have highlighted how children from CARM backgrounds, including those from Indigenous backgrounds, are frequently viewed through a deficit lens in educational settings. For example, citing Malin et al. (1996), Sisson and colleagues highlight that "contemporary Australian education policy and practice is filtered through a 'white' lens that often positions Aboriginal parents and children in deficit terms and requiring intervention" (Sisson et al., 2024 p. 16).

Street's (1984) influential critique of the 'autonomous model of literacy' reveals how supposedly neutral approaches to reading instruction embed white middle-class cultural assumptions about what constitutes legitimate literacy practice. This autonomous model treats literacy as a technical skill divorced from social context, masking how dominant literacy practices reflect and reproduce specific cultural norms. Numerous studies demonstrate how schools often misinterpret cultural and linguistic differences as educational deficits, particularly when evaluating the early literacy experiences of children from non-dominant communities (Compton-Lilly, 2009; Compton-Lilly et al., 2012; Flores & Rosa, 2020; Rosa, 2016; Souto-Manning, 2013; Souto-Manning & Yoon, 2018). Further, foundational ethnographic studies (Barton & Hamilton, 1998; Heath, 1983) established how white middle-class literacy practices became privileged within formal education systems while different communities' sophisticated literacy practices were systematically devalued, particularly those of African American, Indigenous, and multilingual communities (Gilyard, 1991; Morrison et al., 2019; Rigney, 2003; Smitherman, 2021).

The examination of how marginalised children are positioned within deficit frames reveals how certain linguistic practices are privileged over others, reinforcing existing power structures. Washington and Seidenberg (2021) critique the preferencing of "standard" versions of English, noting that these standards were historically defined by "speakers who are white, more highly educated, and of higher socioeconomic status" (p. 28). They observe that "language varieties are linguistically equal, even when they are not socially equal" (p. 27) and caution that "when children take longer to acquire such knowledge, we should not assume that they are less capable learners" (p. 32). When children's home language differs from school expectations, they face additional cognitive demands—navigating not only content knowledge but also linguistic expectations—that are rarely acknowledged in educational settings.

This pattern of privileging certain ways of speaking while devaluing others forms the foundation of what scholars term "raciolinguistic ideologies" (Flores & Rosa, 2020)—perspectives that conflate racial and linguistic difference, interpreting the language practices of racialised communities as deficient regardless of how closely they approximate dominant language forms. Rosa's (2016) analysis of policy documents, teacher evaluations and classroom interactions demonstrated how "raciolinguistic ideologies stigmatize racially minoritized populations" (p. 176), highlighting the systemic nature of this issue. Critical discourse analysis has further illuminated how institutional policies perpetuate linguistic discrimination. Cushing (2021, 2023) and Cushing and Snell's (2023) analyses reveal how school behaviour policies often conflate linguistic variation with misbehaviour, effectively criminalising the language practices of marginalised students. This demonstrates how disciplinary systems routinely police language use through the guise of maintaining behavioural standards.

The concept of 'funds of knowledge' (González et al., 2005; Moll et al., 1992) emerged as a powerful framework for recognising the rich cultural and linguistic resources that minoritised communities bring to their literacy practices, though research continues to show these resources remain largely untapped in formal education settings (Adam et al., 2023; Boutte et al., 2011; Braden et al., 2022; Souto-Manning et al., 2018). Similarly, Hasan and Williams' (1996) research challenged simplistic narratives about a 'literacy gap' by demonstrating that differences between low and high socioeconomic status families were not primarily about access to books or frequency of reading, but rather about the nature of parent–child book interactions. Thus, universal approaches to reading instruction not only overlook the rich diversity of children's linguistic and cultural resources but also risk viewing certain social groups through deficit frames by interpreting their differences as deficiencies. This tension between standardisation and differentiation raises crucial questions about the conceptualisation and implementation of reading instruction in increasingly diverse educational contexts and demands a shift towards asset-based approaches that recognise and build upon the knowledge and experiences all children bring to their literacy learning. Thus, there is a clear need to consider foregrounding asset-based approaches in literacy education.

Asset-Based Approaches to Literacy Instruction

Educational approaches that focus primarily on what children lack—particularly children from culturally and linguistically diverse backgrounds—often fail to recognise and build upon the rich resources these learners bring to literacy development. This section examines how shifting from deficit-based to asset-based perspectives can transform literacy instruction, creating more equitable and effective learning environments while still maintaining rigorous attention to essential reading skills.

Recent scholarship has emphasised the need to broaden conceptions of reading success beyond purely cognitive measures. Researchers, including Muhammad (2020) and Flores (2020), have advocated for approaches that consider the multiple languages and literacies students bring to the classroom and how these can be integrated with evidence-based instruction. This work suggests that truly effective reading instruction must bridge the gap between cognitive science and cultural responsiveness, ensuring that all students see their experiences and ways of knowing reflected in literacy education.

Boutte and colleagues have been particularly influential in challenging deficit perspectives and promoting asset-based approaches to literacy instruction for marginalised students. Johnson et al. (2019) developed their concept of 'revolutionary love' as a response to educational practices that marginalise Black children. They observe that "too many urban schools serve as violent sites that destroy the knowledge and rich cultural practices that Black youth bring to classrooms through privileging the onto-epistemologies and cultural practices of their white counterparts" (p. 49). Building on this foundation, Braden et al. (2022) document successful approaches to implementing Pro-Black teaching in K-3 classrooms. Their research demonstrates how explicit attention to racial and cultural identity within literacy instruction enhances children's engagement with text and development of critical literacy skills. They argue that "all students benefit from an emancipatory Pro-Black curriculum because this type of curriculum creates a paradigm in which they are prepared with a counternarrative to the systemic anti-Blackness present in the 'real world'" (p. 501).

In the Australian context, Indigenous approaches offer powerful frameworks for asset-based literacy instruction. Cumming-Potvin et al. (2022) describe yarning as "an informal, but focused conversation, and a pathway of two-way learning" (p. 1346) that can complement evidence-based instruction while honouring Indigenous ways of knowing. Jackson-Barrett and Lee-Hammond's (2019) research on *On Country Learning* extends this approach by positioning Country as both text and teacher. Their metaphorical journey from 'Pink Floyd to Pink Hill'—from rigid pedagogies to transformative practices grounded in Country—demonstrates how education can "disrupt the historically and socially constructed power positions of educators and the western curriculum" (p. 40). Their work shows how cultural knowledge embedded in Country becomes the foundation for literacy development, with children creating sophisticated representations like maps that demonstrate deep understanding of place while developing essential literacy skills. This exemplifies how transformative approaches honour Indigenous ways of knowing while advancing academic outcomes.

Knight (2024) provides additional insights through his examination of oracy and cultural capital, arguing for understanding spoken language not just as a technical skill but as a means for personal and social transformation encompassing both "personal transformation through 'exploratory' forms of talk and societal transformation through the cultivation of agency and empowerment" (p. 44).

Integrative Models for Practice

Recent literacy research has seen the emergence of promising methodologies that successfully integrate explicit instruction in code-breaking skills with culturally responsive pedagogical approaches. These integrative frameworks acknowledge that effective reading instruction must simultaneously address both the technical aspects of decoding and the broader sociocultural dimensions of literacy acquisition. This integration is particularly important given Allington's (2013) observation that "no research has demonstrated that test prep actually improves performance on standardised tests of reading development, much less fostered improved reading behaviours" (p. 527). This critique highlights how standardised approaches often divert time and resources from more effective, culturally responsive instructional practices that could better serve diverse learners.

Washington and Seidenberg (2021) offer important insights into how such integrative approaches can address the specific needs of children who speak non-dominant language varieties. They emphasise that "teaching children who are becoming bidialectal to read does not require an entirely new, separate theory of reading instruction. The same elements that have been identified for all developing readers to break the code are necessary for children who speak AAE as well. What differs is the delivery of these elements" (p. 40). Their approach is fundamentally about expanding children's linguistic repertoires rather than 'correcting' or 'fixing' their home language. They provide examples of how to adapt phonics instruction for speakers of AAE in ways that honour home language while building additional language resources—such as focusing more explicitly on final consonants that may be less prominent in spoken AAE or providing opportunities to practice different pronunciations across language varieties. Crucially, these adaptations are presented as additions to students' existing linguistic knowledge, not replacements for it. This perspective highlights the need for instructional approaches that acknowledge linguistic diversity as an asset while maintaining high expectations for all learners.

Washington and Seidenberg's approach aligns with the Four Resources Model (Freebody & Luke, 1990) discussed earlier, reinforcing that effective readers need to develop multiple capabilities simultaneously. Their recommendations support children not only as code-breakers (through explicit attention to phonological differences) but also as text users (recognising how language varies across contexts) and text participants (connecting reading to cultural knowledge). Such integrative approaches demonstrate how culturally responsive instruction can strengthen rather than compromise the development of essential literacy skills across all four roles that competent readers must fulfil.

Translanguaging pedagogies represent another significant development in this integrative space. García et al. (2016) documented how such approaches enable multilingual students to draw upon their complete linguistic repertoires when developing both decoding skills and deeper comprehension strategies. Their research, and that of others (Conteh, 2018; García & Kleifgen, 2019; Seltzer & García, 2020), demonstrates that acknowledging and incorporating students' full language capabilities using translanguaging as pedagogy enhances rather than hinders literacy development and:

> …holds much promise to provide minoritised bilingual students… with ways to deepen understanding of texts, generate more diverse texts, enjoy more *confianza* (confidence) as literate beings, and experience a deeper critical multilingual awareness.
> (García & Kleifgen, 2019, p. 16)

A common misconception is that only bilingual teachers can implement translanguaging effectively. However, emerging research demonstrates that monolingual teachers can successfully create translanguaging spaces that honour and leverage students' full linguistic repertoires. Desmond (2024) identifies three key elements that enable monolingual teachers to implement translanguaging effectively: comprehensive teacher preparation; willingness to release linguistic control; and adoption of heteroglossic ideologies that value multilingualism. When monolingual teachers position themselves as co-learners rather than linguistic experts, they create spaces where students' diverse linguistic knowledge becomes a valued classroom resource. This shift in teacher stance is critical. Such teachers create what Stille et al. (2016) describe as a "mirror effect" where "teachers [become] learners, as the teacher teaches and learns from the students" (p. 490). This reciprocal learning relationship transforms classrooms into multilingual spaces where all linguistic resources are valued, regardless of the teacher's own language background. As emphasised in the ACTA/ATESOL roadmap (2022), effective reading instruction for multilingual learners requires both explicit teaching of English-specific decoding skills and creating learning spaces that validate students' home languages and cultural knowledge as valuable resources for meaning-making.

Similarly, Muhammad's (2020) historically responsive literacy framework provides a particularly powerful model for integration in her book *Cultivating Genius*. She demonstrates how Black literary traditions and cultural practices can inform rigorous literacy instruction that simultaneously develops technical skills and critical consciousness. Her framework illustrates that attention to identity development, intellectual growth, critical analysis and skills acquisition should not be conceptualised as competing priorities but rather as complementary and mutually reinforcing elements of comprehensive literacy education. These integrative approaches challenge the false binary that positions culturally responsive teaching as separate from or incompatible with explicit skills instruction. Instead, they demonstrate that instruction in constrained skills like phonics, when thoughtfully embedded within culturally meaningful contexts and practices, becomes both more effective instructionally and more empowering for diverse learners. As Paris and Alim (2017) argue in their work on culturally sustaining pedagogies, the goal is not to replace skills-focused instruction but to ensure that such instruction serves broader educational aims of student self-determination and cultural continuity.

The scholars whose work informs asset-based approaches to literacy instruction represent a spectrum of perspectives about the extent to which educational systems themselves require transformation. While there is broad agreement about the need to value students' linguistic and cultural resources, scholars differ in their emphasis on how to address educational inequities. Some researchers, including Washington and Seidenberg (2021), focus on pragmatic approaches that help children navigate existing educational systems more successfully. Their work highlights how teachers can support students who speak non-dominant language varieties to develop bidialectal fluency, recognising that "speaking AAE is not inherently an obstacle to becoming a reader, but it becomes one when children's specific needs are not recognised or addressed" (p. 30). This perspective acknowledges current systemic realities while offering practical interventions that can help children succeed academically within those systems.

Other scholars, such as Boutte and colleagues (Braden et al., 2022), advocate more explicitly for transformational approaches that challenge the foundations of educational systems themselves. Their work on Pro-Black pedagogies argues not just for better accommodation of linguistic and cultural diversity, but also for fundamental shifts in how schools conceptualise knowledge, literacy and learning. This perspective maintains that "emancipating early childhood literacy curricula" requires confronting and dismantling systemic racism rather than merely helping students adapt to systems that marginalise them.

These perspectives are not necessarily in conflict—rather, they can be viewed as complementary approaches addressing different aspects of the same challenge. Educators committed to equitable literacy instruction may find themselves working simultaneously to help students navigate existing systems while also advocating for more fundamental transformations. The MELLE presented in this book incorporates both the need for practical, evidence-informed approaches that support students' immediate literacy development and the longer-term imperative to transform educational systems so that they genuinely value and build upon the diverse linguistic and cultural resources that all children bring to the classroom.

Connecting to the Model for Equitable Literacy Learning Environments

This critical examination of 'best practice' directly informs the Quality Instruction dimension of the MELLE presented fully in Chapter 7.

Figure 3.2 illustrates how Quality Instruction functions as one of three interconnected dimensions—alongside opportunity to read and representation in reading materials—that together create equitable literacy environments.

Within the MELLE framework, Quality Instruction encompasses:

- Evidence-informed code-breaking practices grounded in cognitive science
- Attention to both constrained skills (phonics, phonemic awareness) and unconstrained skills (vocabulary, fluency, comprehension, critical literacy)
- Development of all four resources identified by Freebody and Luke—code-breaking, meaning-making, text use and text criticism—which forms the theoretical foundation of the MELLE as discussed earlier

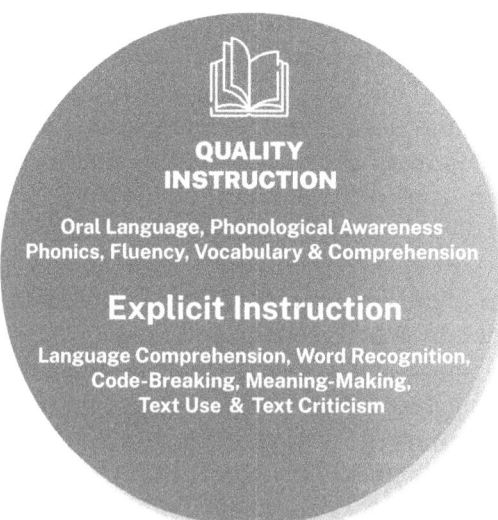

Figure 3.2 Quality instruction in the MELLE.

- Pedagogical approaches drawn from sociocultural research on culturally responsive teaching
- Instructional strategies that build upon children's existing linguistic and cultural resources

This integrated perspective aligns with diverse international frameworks, including the Four Resources Model (Freebody & Luke, 1990), systematic phonics instruction and critical literacy development. The asset-based approaches discussed in the preceding section are central to this dimension, recognising that effective instruction leverages children's cultural knowledge rather than attempting to replace it.

Conclusion

This chapter has challenged the often-prevailing notion that standardised approaches derived primarily from cognitive science research can adequately address the literacy needs of diverse student populations. While cognitive science provides essential insights into reading development, these insights must be contextualised within broader understandings that acknowledge the complex relationships between language, identity, power and literacy learning. Creating equitable reading environments requires moving beyond the restrictive binary that has characterised the reading wars. Quality instruction must integrate explicit teaching of foundational skills with approaches that recognise and build upon the rich linguistic and cultural resources that all children bring to the classroom. This integration is not merely a matter of changing individual teacher practices but also requires transformation of policies, assessment approaches and institutional structures that currently privilege white middle-class ways of knowing and being.

The empirical evidence presented throughout this chapter demonstrates that approaches honouring both technical literacy skills across all four resources identified by Freebody and Luke (1990)—code-breaking, meaning-making, text using, and text analysis—and cultural responsiveness yield the strongest outcomes for all learners, particularly those from marginalised communities. This evidence forms the foundation for the Quality Instruction dimension of the MELLE framework, emphasising that effective reading instruction must be both rigorous and responsive to children's diverse backgrounds and experiences. However, as the following chapter will explore, even the most culturally responsive instruction cannot fully address literacy inequities when children lack equitable opportunities to engage with diverse texts. As Allington (2013) notes, "struggling readers…do far less reading than good readers" (p. 527). Chapter 4 will examine how opportunity disparities compound instructional challenges, further illuminating why a comprehensive approach to equitable literacy education must address not only how children are taught to read, but also what opportunities they have to develop as engaged, critical readers.

References

ACTA/ATESOL. (2022). *A Roadmap for Supporting English Language Development in Australian Schools*. Australian Council of TESOL Associations and Applied Linguistics Association of Australia.

Adam, H., Barblett, L., Kirk, G., & Boutte, G. S. (2023). (Re)considering equity, inclusion and belonging in the updating of the Early Years Learning Framework for Australia: The potential and pitfalls of book sharing. *Contemporary Issues in Early Childhood, 24*(2), 189–207. https://doi.org/10.1177/14639491231176897

Allington, R. L. (2013). What really matters when working with struggling readers. *The Reading Teacher, 66*(7), 520–530. https://doi.org/10.1002/TRTR.1154

Barton, D., & Hamilton, M. (1998). *Local Literacies: Reading and Writing in One Community*. Routledge.

Boutte, G. S., Lopez-Robertson, J., & Powers-Costello, E. (2011). Moving beyond colorblindness in early childhood classrooms. *Early Childhood Education Journal, 39*(5), 335–342. https://doi.org/10.1007/s10643-011-0457-x

Braden, E., Boutte, G., Wynter-Hoyte, K., Long, S., Aitken, C., Collins, S., Frazier, J., Gamble, E., Hall, L., Hodge, S., McDonald, C., Merritt, A., Mosso-Taylor, S., Samuel, K., Stout, C., Tafel, J., Warren, T., & Witherspoon, J. (2022). Emancipating early childhood literacy curricula: Pro-Black teaching in K-3 classrooms. *Journal of Early Childhood Literacy, 22*(4), 500–539. https://doi.org/10.1177/14687984221135488

Castles, A., Rastle, K., & Nation, K. (2018). Ending the reading wars: Reading acquisition from novice to expert. *Psychological Science in the Public Interest, 19*(1), 5–51. https://doi.org/10.1177/1529100618772271

Comber, B. (2015). Critical literacy and social justice. *Journal of Adolescent & Adult Literacy, 58*(5), 362–367. https://doi.org/10.1002/jaal.370

Comber, B., & Woods, A. (2018). Pedagogies of belonging in literacy classrooms and beyond: What's holding us back? In C. Halse (Ed.), *Interrogating Belonging for Young People in Schools* (pp. 263–281). Palgrave Macmillan.

Compton-Lilly, C. (2009). *Breaking the Silence: Recognising the Social and Cultural Resources Students Bring to the Classroom*. International Reading Association.

Compton-Lilly, C., Rogers, R., & Lewis, T. Y. (2012). Analyzing epistemological considerations related to diversity: An integrative critical literature review of family literacy scholarship. *Reading Research Quarterly, 47*(1), 33–60. https://doi.org/10.1002/RRQ.009

Conteh, J. (2018). Translanguaging as pedagogy: A critical review. In A. Creese & A. Blackledge (Eds.), *The Routledge Handbook of Language and Superdiversity*. Routledge.

Cumming-Potvin, W., Jackson-Barrett, L., & Potvin, D. (2022). Aboriginal perspectives matter: Yarning and reflecting about teaching literacies with multimodal Aboriginal texts. *Issues in Educational Research, 32*(4), 1342–1363.

Cushing, I. (2021). *Standards, Stigma, Surveillance: Raciolinguistic Ideologies and England's Schools*. Palgrave Macmillan.

Cushing, I. (2023). Word rich or word poor? Deficit discourses, raciolinguistic ideologies and the resurgence of the 'word gap' in England's education policy. *Critical Inquiry in Language Studies, 20*(4), 305–331. https://doi.org/10.1080/15427587.2022.2102014

Cushing, I., & Snell, J. (2023). The (white) ears of Ofsted: A raciolinguistic perspective on the listening practices of the schools inspectorate. *Language in Society, 52*(1), 363–386. https://doi.org/10.1017/S0047404522000094

Dehaene, S. (2009). *Reading in the Brain: The Science and Evolution of a Human Invention*. Viking.

Desmond, W. (2024). Translanguaging and the monolingual teacher: Leveraging students' full linguistic competencies within literacy development. *ORTESOL Journal, 41*, 4–20.

Dobrescu, I., Holden, R. J., Motta, A., Piccoli, A., Roberts, P., & Walker, S. (2022). Cultural context in standardized tests. *UNSW Economics Working Paper*, 2021-08. https://doi.org/10.2139/ssrn.3983663

Duke, N. K., & Cartwright, K. B. (2021). The science of reading progresses: Communicating advances beyond the simple view of reading. *Reading Research Quarterly, 56*(S1), S25–S44. https://doi.org/10.1002/rrq.411

Ehri, L. C. (2020). The science of learning to read words: A case for systematic phonics instruction. *Reading Research Quarterly, 55*(S1), S45–S60. https://doi.org/10.1002/rrq.334

Ehri, L. C. (2023). Roads travelled researching how children learn to read words. *Australian Journal of Learning Difficulties, 28*(1), 55–71. https://doi.org/10.1080/19404158.2023.2208164

Flores, N. (2020). From academic language to language architecture: Challenging raciolinguistic ideologies in research and practice. *Theory Into Practice, 59*(1), 22–31. https://doi.org/10.1080/00405841.2019.1665411

Flores, N., & Rosa, J. (2020). Bringing race into second language acquisition. *The Modern Language Journal, 104*(S1), 145–151. https://doi.org/10.1111/modl.12523

Freebody, P., & Luke, A. (1990). Literacies programs: Debates and demands in cultural context. *Prospect: Australian Journal of TESOL, 5*(3), 7–16.

García, O., Johnson, S. I., & Seltzer, K. (2016). *The Translanguaging Classroom: Leveraging Student Bilingualism for Learning*. Brookes Publishing Co.

García, O., & Kleifgen, J. A. (2019). Translanguaging and literacies. *Reading Research Quarterly, 55*(4), 553–571. https://doi.org/10.1002/rrq.286

Gilyard, K. (1991). *Voices of the Self: A Study of Language Competence*. Wayne State University Press.

González, N., Moll, L. C., & Amanti, C. (Eds.) (2005). *Funds of Knowledge: Theorising Practices in Households, Communities, and Classrooms*. Lawrence Erlbaum Associates.

Gough, P. B., & Tunmer, W. E. (1986). Decoding, reading, and reading disability. *Remedial and Special Education, 7*(1), 6–10. https://doi.org/10.1177/074193258600700104

Gutiérrez, K. D., & Larson, J. (1994). Language borders: Recitation as hegemonic discourse. *International Journal of Educational Reform, 3*(1), 22–36.

Hasan, R., & Williams, G. (1996). *Literacy in Society*. Longman.

Heath, S. B. (1983). *Ways with Words: Language, Life, and Work in Communities and Classrooms*. Cambridge University Press.

Hoover, W. A., & Tunmer, W. E. (2020). *The Cognitive Foundations of Reading and Its Acquisition: A Framework with Applications Connecting Teaching and Learning*. Springer. https://doi.org/10.1007/978-3-030-44195-1

Jackson-Barrett, E. M., & Lee-Hammond, L. (2019). From Pink Floyd to Pink Hill: Transforming education from the bricks in the wall to the connections of country in remote aboriginal education. *Australian Journal of Teacher Education, 44*(10). https://doi.org/10.14221/ajte.2019v44n10.3

Johnson, L. L., Bryan, N., & Boutte, G. S. (2019). Show us the love: Revolutionary teaching in (un)critical times. *Urban Review: Issues and Ideas in Public Education*, *51*(1), 46–64.

Knight, R. (2024). Oracy and cultural capital: The transformative potential of spoken language. *Literacy*, *58*(1), 37–47. https://doi.org/10.1111/lit.12343

Konza, D. (2014). Teaching reading: Why the "Fab five" should be the "Big six". *Australian Journal of Teacher Education (Online)*, *39*(12), 153–169. https://doi.org/10.14221/ajte.2014v39n12.10

López, F. A. (2016). Culturally responsive pedagogies in Arizona and Latino students' achievement. *Teachers College Record*, *118*(5), 1–42. https://doi.org/10.1177/016146811611800503

Luke, A., & Freebody, P. (1999). A map of possible practices: Further notes on the four resources model. *Practically Primary*, *4*(2), 5–8.

Malin, M., Campbell, K., & Agius, L. (1996). Raising children in the Nunga Aboriginal Way. *Family Matters*, *43*, 43–47.

Martinez, R. A. (2018). Beyond the english learner label: Recognizing the richness of bi/multilingual students' linguistic repertoires. *The Reading Teacher*, *71*(5), 515–522. https://doi.org/10.1002/trtr.1679

Moll, L. C., Amanti, C., Neff, D., & Gonzalez, N. (1992). Funds of knowledge for teaching: Using a qualitative approach to connect homes and classrooms. *Theory into Practice*, *31*(2), 132–141.

Morrison, A., Rigney, L.-I., Hattam, R., & Diplock, A. (2019). *Toward an Australian Culturally Responsive Pedagogy: A Narrative Review of the Literature*. University of South Australia.

Muhammad, G. (2020). *Cultivating Genius: An Equity Framework for Culturally and Historically Responsive Literacy*. Scholastic. https://doi.org/10.1177/00420859231162897

National Inquiry into the Teaching of Literacy. (2005). *Teaching Reading: Report and Recommendations*. Australian Government Department of Education, Science and Training.

National Reading Panel. (2000). *Teaching Children to Read: An Evidence-Based Assessment of the Scientific Research Literature and Its Implications for Reading Instruction*. National Institute of Child Health and Human Development.

Paris, D., & Alim, H. S. (Eds.). (2017). *Culturally Sustaining Pedagogies: Teaching and Learning for Justice in a Changing World*. Teachers College Press.

Rigney, L-I. (2003). Indigenous education, languages and treaty: The redefinition of a new relationship with Australia. In *Treaty: Let's get it Right!* (pp. 72–87). Aboriginal Studies Press.

Rosa, J. (2016). Standardization, racialization, languagelessness: Raciolinguistic ideologies across communicative contexts. *Journal of Linguistic Anthropology*, *26*(2), 162–183. https://doi.org/10.1111/jola.12116

Rose, J. (2006). *Independent Review of the Teaching of Early Reading: Final Report*. Department for Education and Skills.

Scarborough, H. S. (2001). Connecting early language and literacy to later reading (dis)abilities: Evidence, theory, and practice. In S. Neuman & D. Dickinson (Eds.), *Handbook for Research in Early Literacy* (pp. 97–110). Guilford Press.

Seidenberg, M. S. (2017). *Language at the Speed of Sight: How We Read, Why So Many Can't, and What Can Be Done About It*. Basic Books.

Seidenberg, M. S. (2024). Where does the science of reading approach go from here? Paper. University of Wisconsin-Madison.

Seidenberg, M. S., Cooper Borkenhagen, M., & Kearns, D. M. (2020). Lost in translation? Challenges in connecting reading science and educational practice. *Reading Research Quarterly*, 55(S1), S119–S130. https://doi.org/10.1002/rrq.341

Seltzer, K., & García, O. (2020). Broadening the view: Taking up a translanguaging pedagogy with all language-minoritised students. In Z. Tian, L. Aghai, P. Sayer, & J. L. Schissel (Eds.), *Envisioning TESOL Through a Translanguaging Lens* (pp. 23–42). Springer.

Sisson, J. H., Rigney, L. I., Hattam, R., & Morrison, A. (2024). Co-constructed engagement with Australian Aboriginal families in early childhood education. *Teachers and Teaching: Theory and Practice*, 31(1), 16–30. https://doi.org/10.1080/13540602.2024.2328014

Smitherman, G. (2021). *Word from the Mother: Language and African Americans*. Routledge.

Souto-Manning, M. (2013). *Multicultural Teaching in the Early Childhood Classroom: Approaches, Strategies, and Tools, Preschool-2nd Grade*. Teachers College Press.

Souto-Manning, M., Boardman, A., Llerena, C., Martell, J., & Salas, A. (2018). *No More Culturally Irrelevant Teaching*. Heinemann.

Souto-Manning, M., & Yoon, H. S. (2018). *Rethinking Early Literacies: Reading and Rewriting Worlds*. Routledge.

Stille, S.V., Bethke, R., Bradley-Brown, J., Giberson, J., & Hall, G. (2016). Broadening educational practice to include translanguaging: An outcome of educator inquiry into multilingual students' learning needs. *Canadian Modern Language Review*, 72(4), 480–503. https://doi.org/10.3138/cmlr.3432

Street, B. V. (1984). *Literacy in Theory and Practice*. Cambridge University Press.

Tunmer, W., & Hoover, W. (2019). The cognitive foundations of learning to read: A framework for preventing and remediating reading difficulties. *Australian Journal of Learning Difficulties*, 24(1), 75–93. https://doi.org/10.1080/19404158.2019.1614081

Washington, J. A., & Seidenberg, M. S. (2021). Teaching reading to African American children: When home and school language differ. *American Educator*, 45(2), 26–33.

Opportunity Inequities in Access to Reading

4

Introduction: Understanding Opportunity Inequities

Before addressing the lack of opportunity for book access that some children face, it is essential to again consider the systemic opportunity inequities experienced by many children from economically disadvantaged backgrounds, often including those from many Indigenous and Culturally and Racially Marginalised (CARM) communities. As with Chapter 3, this section challenges prevalent deficit perspectives and reframes understandings of literacy through the lens of educational debt rather than achievement gaps.

Rich Literacy Practices Beyond School-Based Definitions

Across diverse cultural and economic contexts, families engage in rich literacy practices that may not align with conventional school-based definitions but are nonetheless valuable and important. This misalignment between home and school literacy practices has been well-documented by researchers examining diverse communities. Compton-Lilly (2007) and Boutte and Compton-Lilly (2022) have extensively studied how families navigate complex literacy practices even when faced with economic challenges, highlighting that all communities possess valuable 'funds of knowledge' that often go unrecognised by educational institutions. Their work, and that of others, challenges deficit perspectives that focus on what children supposedly lack

DOI: 10.4324/9781003628217-4

and instead recognises and celebrates the rich, diverse literacies that exist in all homes. For diverse cultural groups, literacy encompasses much more than school-based reading and writing practices. Indigenous literacy practices, for example, involve rich storytelling traditions, connection to Country, and sophisticated knowledge systems that have been sustained for tens of thousands of years (Lowell et al., 2018; Rennie, 2016). Similarly, Braden et al. (2022) advocate for approaches to literacy education that recognise the importance of culturally relevant teaching practices and materials, arguing that by centring diverse experiences, identities and literacies in the curriculum, educators can create more inclusive and equitable learning environments that affirm rather than marginalise students. Further, Grieshaber et al. (2012), in their Australian pilot study of family literacy practices, challenge the deterministic relationship often assumed between socioeconomic status and home literacy environments. Their findings add to the growing evidence that income is not necessarily directly related to home literacy resources or how those resources are used, and that print resources in the home may not be a reliable indicator of literacy engagement.

From Achievement Gaps to Educational Debt

This more expansive understanding of literacy calls for reframing the challenges faced by children from marginalised communities. Ladson-Billings (2006) articulates a powerful reframing from 'achievement gaps' to 'educational debt', shifting focus from children's perceived deficiencies to society's historical, economic, sociopolitical and moral failures to provide equitable educational opportunities for all children. This reframing has profound implications for how society understands and addresses inequities in education, including access to books and reading opportunities. The concept of educational debt acknowledges that systemic inequities in access to educational resources—not deficits in home literacy environments—are what create disparities in opportunity. Many children across the developed world face inequitable and systemic impacts of poverty on their development, their access to health and learning resources, and, ultimately, on their preparedness for formal learning.

When families are struggling to provide basic needs, they simply cannot allocate resources to books. The emotional response from practitioners working in this field underscores the urgency of addressing these inequities. As one member of the Diverse Books for All Coalition in the USA stated during my Churchill Fellowship, "the kids who most need books, can't afford them," followed by another coalition member's passionate declaration: "we are outraged, this is urgent!" (Adam, 2023). These perspectives from researchers and practitioners converge to highlight a critical point: the opportunity inequity in access to books and reading is not simply an educational issue but also a matter of social justice. It requires a reconsideration of how society, through equitable education and resource allocation, can begin to repay the educational debt owed to children from marginalised communities.

The Impact of Socioeconomic Disparities on Reading

Poverty and Child Development

Across the developed world, children experience significant rates of poverty. In Australia, 17% of children live in poverty (Poverty & Inequality, 2024). In the US, 17% children under five live in poverty (Children's Defense Fund, 2023), while in the UK, an alarming 31% of children face this challenge (Adams, 2025). However, it is crucial to emphasise that these findings do not suggest that children from low-income communities have deficient literacy or language practices. Rather, as Boutte and Compton-Lilly (2022) argue, there is a fundamental misalignment between the types of literacy valued in school settings and the rich literacy practices that exist in many homes. What is measured and valued in educational assessments often reflects dominant cultural practices rather than the diverse ways in which literacy is enacted across different communities.

However, evidence shows poverty has a profound impact on neural development, particularly during early childhood when rapid brain growth occurs. Children raised in low-income environments often experience chronic stress from factors like food insecurity, limited access to healthcare and unstable living conditions, which can disrupt typical neural development and affect areas of the brain related to memory, emotional regulation and executive function (Blair & Raver, 2016). Socioeconomic disparities have also been linked to smaller surface area in brain areas responsible for language, reading and cognitive control, ultimately affecting academic performance and mental health outcomes (Hair et al., 2015; Noble et al., 2015; Sun et al., 2023), setting the stage for challenges that may perpetuate a cycle of disadvantage into adulthood. Further, recent research from England suggests that a third of school staff report "physical underdevelopment" in children who live in poverty (Adams, 2025).

Importantly, recent evidence from Sun et al., while finding similar evidence of poverty and brain development, found that reading for pleasure from a young age can help counteract these effects (Sun et al., 2023). This research examined data from over 10,000 young adolescents and found children who began reading for pleasure early in life showed improved cognition, better mental health and stronger brain development regardless of socioeconomic status. This presents us with a troubling paradox: children living in poverty would benefit greatly from reading for pleasure, but these same children are often deprived of books due to financial constraints.

The Compounding Issue of Race and Systemic Racism

Many children from Indigenous and CARM backgrounds are disproportionately represented in lower socioeconomic (SES) communities. However, assumptions of a universal correlation of poverty and race are ill-informed and harmful (Gorski, 2017; Rudolph, 2019). Further, such perceptions and biases can lead to narratives, often reinforced through media, such as poverty being the result of lack of effort, and perceptions that some marginalised groups or races may be poor because they don't help themselves (Weinstein et al., 2020). Evidence shows that such implicit bias is known to drive misconceptions and labelling of people from CARM and Indigenous backgrounds, with Shirodkar claiming:

> The data could potentially explain why Indigenous Australians continue to experience some of the poorest socioeconomic conditions and living standards in this country—not necessarily through fault on the part of Indigenous Australians, but rather perhaps because of the lens the rest of Australia may view them through.
>
> (Shirodkar, 2019, p. 3)

However, once a child is in school, disparities of poverty and race do not magically disappear. The impacts of poverty on reading outcomes are well known, with standardised test scores and lower educational attainment consistently being correlated with poverty (Hair et al., 2015). In Australia, analysis of annual testing data of Australia's National Assessment of Progress in Literacy and Numeracy (NAPLAN), "found significant achievement gaps in literacy and numeracy between rich and poor students at all year levels, to the equivalent of five years of learning by Year 9" (Cassidy, 2023). In addition, evidence shows the longer children live in poverty the greater the disparity in academic outcomes (Hair et al., 2015).

Further, poorer children and many children from Indigenous and CARM backgrounds continue to be disproportionately impacted by many education practices and policies. This can include disproportionate identification for intervention programmes (Cormier, 2023, 2024) and, especially in the case of children from CARM and Indigenous backgrounds, greater likelihood of being involved in suspensions and exclusions than children from other demographic groups. In the USA "Black, Latinx, and Native American students experience more suspensions and exclusions as compared to other demographic groups, although they do not display more problematic behavior" (Harms & Garrett-Ruffin, 2023, p. 50). These systemic overrepresentations are also seen in Australia. The New South Wales Department of Education *Student Behaviour Strategy* of 2021 highlights the overrepresentation in suspensions and exclusions of "students with disability, Aboriginal students, students in rural and remote areas and students experiencing socio-economic disadvantage" (New South Wales Department of Education, 2021, p. 7). Thus, the students often in most need of rich, high-quality educational experiences to mitigate impacts of poverty and oppression are, in fact, those most likely to be excluded from those same experiences, further compounding the systemic inequities and educational outcomes for these children. This perpetuates the 'education debt' (Ladson-Billings, 2006)—the accumulated disadvantage and disinvestment in the education of poor students and students of colour that has persisted over generations. Addressing this debt requires more than just high-quality teaching; it demands systemic change at every level of society, including in how provision and access to books and reading opportunities.

As highlighted earlier, the impact of poverty on educational outcomes creates a reciprocal disadvantage that cannot be overlooked. If reading can help limit the impact of poverty on educational outcomes, as Sun et al. and others suggest, then books must be accessible to all families regardless of financial circumstances. Provision of books should be part of front-line systemic support for families. Without this, children from impoverished backgrounds will continue to be targeted for intervention programmes as soon as they enter formal education.

The Literacy Myth: Reading Instruction and Socioeconomic Reality

A recurring narrative around the teaching of reading is the misconception that teaching a child to read will future-proof them against a lifetime of poverty. This narrative, which Graff (1979, 2010) famously termed 'The Literacy

Myth,' represents a reductionist viewpoint of literacy's value and overstates its power to alleviate poverty. As discussed in Chapter 3 regarding the limitations of standardised approaches to reading instruction, Brian Street's (1984) critique of the 'autonomous model' of literacy reminds us that reading skills do not automatically confer economic benefits regardless of social context. This oversimplification creates several problematic consequences for education. First, it places unfair expectations on teachers, positioning them as solely responsible for economic outcomes that extend far beyond classroom walls. Pauline Lipman's (2004) influential work *High Stakes Education* demonstrated how economic determinism in literacy policies fundamentally misunderstands the complex relationship between education and poverty. Her research revealed how economic structures themselves create boundaries that limit literacy's power to address poverty—yet policies continue to reflect an underlying assumption that teaching reading is sufficient to overcome socioeconomic disadvantage.

The reality is considerably more nuanced: teaching a child from a disadvantaged background to read means they can read—it does not mean they will no longer experience poverty. When governments claim that teaching children to read is the answer to poverty, they effectively neglect their responsibility to address the root causes of systemic inequity through comprehensive social and economic policies. Heath's (1983) ethnographic research in *Ways with Words* provides compelling evidence for this perspective, demonstrating how literacy practices are deeply embedded in community contexts, and how simplistic notions about literacy acquisition leading directly to economic outcomes fail to account for these sociocultural complexities. Stephen Ball's (2012) critical work on neoliberal education policies further illuminates how literacy is often positioned as a technical solution to economic problems while systemic issues remain unaddressed. This framing creates a dangerous cycle: when the focus is placed solely on reading outcomes without addressing children's impoverished circumstances, teachers become scapegoats, blamed for poor literacy outcomes and thus portrayed as contributing to the very prevalence of poverty they are tasked with solving through literacy instruction.

What is often overlooked in these discussions is the compounding nature of educational advantage and disadvantage over time. Stanovich's (1986) research on the 'Matthew Effect' in reading demonstrates how initial reading advantages or disadvantages multiply throughout children's educational journeys, with socioeconomic factors playing a crucial role in determining these initial conditions. Children who begin school with little to no access to books at home typically continue to experience limited access throughout their education. This continuity of disadvantage helps explain why achievement disparities not only persist but widen—children from disadvantaged backgrounds often start behind their peers and, despite school-based interventions, fall increasingly further behind as educational demands increase. While literacy is unquestionably important, it represents just one factor among many affecting economic outcomes, and structural factors often predominate in determining life chances. This complex reality underscores why literacy instruction alone cannot resolve entrenched educational inequities without concurrent efforts to address the underlying socioeconomic conditions that shape children's lives and learning opportunities. This will be further examined in Chapter 9.

Barriers to Reading Opportunity

The Role of Libraries and Access to Books

School, classroom and local libraries serve as crucial access points to books for many children, particularly those experiencing economic disadvantage. My Churchill Fellowship investigation revealed concerning patterns in library provision and funding across several developed nations.

The American educational landscape presents a troubling picture. More than 8,830 public schools operate without any library facilities whatsoever, while approximately 17,000 schools with libraries lack professionally qualified librarians (American Library Association, 2022). This situation is particularly concerning given the strong evidence base supporting well-resourced libraries' positive impact on educational outcomes. A comprehensive analysis of 34 statewide studies demonstrated that schools with certified librarians produce students with superior standardised test results, enhanced digital and information literacy capabilities, and higher graduation rates compared to institutions without professional library staff (Lance & Kachel, 2018). Beyond these resource challenges, mounting pressure from organised parent groups and political organisations seeking to restrict access to books representing diverse perspectives has resulted in widespread book removals, sometimes contravening schools' own established policies.

In Britain, the context differs somewhat, with no centralised mandate or dedicated funding stream for school libraries. Educational leadership teams retain complete discretion regarding library provision within their institutions. Approximately 14% of UK schools operate without dedicated library facilities, with a clear socioeconomic dimension to this issue (Great School Libraries Campaign, 2023). Schools in economically disadvantaged communities are significantly less likely to maintain libraries than those in more affluent areas, and existing libraries typically contain fewer resources. Institutions with higher percentages of pupils eligible for free school meals are more than twice as likely to lack library facilities or qualified librarians compared to schools serving more economically advantaged populations (Great School Libraries Campaign, 2023).

While Australian schools generally maintain libraries, significant disparities exist in their resourcing and staffing. Inadequate funding and insufficient numbers of qualified teacher-librarians emerge as primary concerns in Softlink's recurring national survey of school libraries. Smaller primary schools and those in geographically remote locations typically operate with significantly reduced library budgets compared to larger, urban, and high-SES institutions (Softlink Education, 2024). With annual school library budget allocations ranging from less than $1,000 AUD to over $50,000 AUD, pronounced inequities in resource provision disproportionately affect schools serving economically disadvantaged and culturally diverse communities. A concerning trend of schools—particularly those in disadvantaged areas—eliminating professional teacher-librarian positions in favour of library officers or educational assistants who typically lack specialised expertise further compromises literacy development and information skills (Merga, 2019).

This reduction, underfunding or absence of school libraries represents a significant systemic inequity that intensifies the effects of economic disadvantage. Children who already have minimal access to books at home frequently encounter similar limitations at school, creating a compounding disadvantage that inevitably influences their reading development and broader educational outcomes. As the Great School Libraries Campaign (2023) aptly states, "it is unacceptable that children experiencing today's education system are at the whim of their region, postcode or school demographic when it comes to reading and learning provision." Michael Rosen, renowned author, poet and former UK Children's Laureate, advocates for these findings to serve as an urgent call to action for government intervention:

> We have countless examples of research showing that children who read for pleasure widely and often are best able to benefit from what education offers. Berating parents, children or teachers for 'failing' will solve nothing. It [improving reading levels] needs full government backing, with as much money and effort as they put into compulsory phonics teaching, to support schools and communities in this.
>
> (Ferguson, 2020)

Limited Opportunities for Reading for Pleasure

Many classrooms and schools impose significant limitations on children's opportunities to read for pleasure (RfP), often also known by terms such as Independent Reading (IR), Free Voluntary Reading (FVR) and Independent Silent Reading (ISR). This constraint exists despite substantial evidence supporting its importance for literacy development and overall educational outcomes. The restricted time for reading for pleasure stems largely from what educators term a 'crowded curriculum,' whereby instructional time for core learning areas leaves little room for children to select and engage with books independently, or for teachers to read to them.

The Critical Role of Reading Volume and Teacher Read-Alouds

Research consistently demonstrates that reading volume directly influences literacy development across multiple dimensions. The quantity of text students read serves as a critical factor in developing reading fluency, vocabulary and comprehension skills, with time spent reading standing as one of the strongest predictors of reading achievement (Allington, 2014). This relationship between volume and proficiency creates a compelling case for prioritising opportunities for children to engage extensively with texts.

Within this context, book sharing or read-aloud practices by educators emerge as particularly vital in early years education. These experiences allow teachers to introduce books that may exceed children's independent reading abilities but provide rich content for discussion, comprehension and vocabulary development, and deeper understanding of texts, significantly influencing children's motivation to read independently. However, my doctoral research revealed concerning inequities in the implementation of these practices. Kindergarten children generally were not receiving the amount of shared book time recommended by experts, with children in disadvantaged areas receiving less than half the book-sharing time—and even less high-quality book sharing—than those in more affluent areas (Adam & Barratt-Pugh, 2020). This disparity unintentionally reinforces barriers to academic success for already marginalised children, particularly those from Aboriginal and other CARM communities.

The importance of these reading opportunities extends beyond skill development to encompass the motivational dimensions of reading. As Duke et al. (2021, p. 667) emphasise, "Scientific research has shown that motivation for reading is an(other) important determinant of reading comprehension, one that we ignore at our peril." This connection between motivation and achievement underscores why opportunities for engaging with personally meaningful texts are essential to comprehensive literacy education.

Reading for Pleasure: Educational Practice, Not Just Fun

The significant research contributions of Cremin and colleagues have transformed understanding of reading for pleasure from a peripheral activity to an essential educational practice with substantial cognitive benefits. Children who engage in pleasure reading make greater progress in vocabulary, spelling and mathematics, demonstrate enhanced text comprehension and grammar, and develop more positive attitudes towards reading (Cremin, 2019). Beyond these individual benefits, Cremin and Scholes' comprehensive international review illuminates the complex relationship between voluntary reading and academic achievement, highlighting how the strength of these relationships varies across cultural contexts and demographics. This variation suggests the need for contextually responsive approaches rather than 'one-size-fits-all' implementations (Cremin & Scholes, 2024).

TEACHER PRACTICE AND READING FOR PLEASURE PEDAGOGIES

Beyond establishing the importance of reading for pleasure, research has identified specific 'reading for pleasure pedagogies' that create vibrant reading communities in classrooms. These include creating social reading environments rich in diverse texts, providing regular opportunities for book discussions, supporting children's agency in selecting reading materials, developing rich knowledge of children's literature and fostering reciprocal reading communities that promote meaningful interactions around texts (Cremin et al., 2014; Cremin & Scholes, 2024). Notably, teachers who themselves read for pleasure and possess extensive knowledge of children's literature are better equipped to recommend appropriate texts and engage in authentic discussions about books—suggesting that professional development should enhance teachers' personal reading practices and literary knowledge rather than merely focusing on instructional techniques (Hendry et al., 2025).

INSTITUTIONAL BARRIERS TO READING FOR PLEASURE

Despite this robust evidence base, reading for pleasure frequently encounters institutional resistance in educational settings. A recurring theme throughout my Churchill Fellowship and in my ongoing work with educators is that teachers often must defend time allocated to reading for pleasure to school leadership. This pressure to justify an evidence-based practice reveals deeper systemic tensions between assessment-driven policies and comprehensive literacy education. The practical impact of these barriers appears in troubling statistics: Scholastics' biennial *Kids and Family Reading Report* for 2019 showed only 17% of school-aged children surveyed reported having daily opportunities to read self-selected books at school, whilst 30% of six-to-eight-year-olds stated this never occurred (Scholastic, 2019). More recent data shows the percentage of children who read 5–7 days weekly has declined from 37% in 2010 to 28% in 2024, with over half of children who attend schools without libraries reporting difficulty finding books (Scholastic, 2024).

The Narrowing Curriculum and Digital Divide

This restriction of reading for pleasure opportunities reflects broader trends in educational policy and practice, particularly the intensifying focus on skills-based literacy instruction within environments emphasising high-stakes testing and accountability. Research from the UK demonstrates that while teachers recognised the value of reading for pleasure, they struggle to prioritise it amidst crowded curriculum demands and assessment pressures (Cremin et al., 2014).

Access to reading materials is further complicated by inequities in digital resources. In today's increasingly digital landscape, children from low-income backgrounds often face a 'digital divide'—they are less likely to have access to digital devices, high-speed internet and adult guidance in navigating digital literacy resources. This digital divide directly impacts children's access to ebooks, digital libraries and online reading platforms that could otherwise supplement limited physical book collections. These disparities were intensified by the COVID-19 pandemic (Chamberlain et al., 2022; Sanders & Scanlon, 2021). The Australian Digital Inclusion Index highlights significant disparity in digital access based on socioeconomic status, geographic location and Indigenous status (Thomas et al., 2023), with schools serving disadvantaged communities often having less access to up-to-date technologies and fewer staff with expertise in digital literacy pedagogy.

These dual challenges—restricted time for reading engagement and inequitable access to both print and digital texts—combine to create significant barriers to literacy development for many children, particularly those from disadvantaged backgrounds. Recent evidence underscores the urgency of addressing these constraints, with UK children's attitudes towards reading for pleasure reaching their lowest point since 2005 and the number of young people reporting reading in their spare time halving since 2019 to just 34.6% (Hendry et al., 2025). Particularly concerning is what researchers term a 'levelling-down' effect, whereby the decline in reading engagement among more advantaged children has been steeper than for disadvantaged children—suggesting a broader engagement crisis affecting children across all socioeconomic levels rather than simply an access issue.

Restricting Choice: The Problem of Limiting Children's Reading Options

Beyond time constraints, another problematic practice in many schools involves restricting children's book choices based on perceived reading ability. This approach prevents children from accessing books deemed 'too challenging' or above their assigned reading levels. Such limitations, whilst perhaps well-intentioned, can significantly undermine children's motivation and development as readers.

Shanahan (2020) presents a compelling argument against restricting children to books they can already read independently, pointing out that such constraints fundamentally reduce children's opportunities to learn and develop as readers. Whilst instructional-level reading serves important purposes in structured literacy lessons, children benefit substantially from exposure to, and engagement with, a wide range of texts, including those that might initially appear challenging when approached independently. Research by Hempel-Jorgensen et al. (2018) reveals that children's reading identities and engagement are significantly influenced by the freedom to choose texts and the social dimensions of reading. Their study found that when children experienced greater agency in reading choices and had opportunities to discuss books with peers, they developed more positive reading identities and demonstrated stronger engagement with texts. These findings further support the argument that reading for pleasure should be integrated into the school day rather than positioned exclusively as a home-based activity.

Towards an Integrated Approach: Complementary, Not Competing Priorities

The tension between dedicating time to explicit reading instruction versus providing opportunities for reading for pleasure remains an active debate in literacy education. Proponents of evidence-based reading instruction often argue that reading for pleasure should not replace instructional time focused on developing reading skills (Shanahan, 2024). Similarly, Fisher and

Frey (2018) suggest that whilst comprehensive reading instruction should encompass diverse reading experiences, independent reading should be encouraged beyond the classroom rather than incorporated into everyday instruction.

However, recent meta-analyses provide compelling evidence for including reading for pleasure within educational settings. While noting the importance of instructional time, Bus et al. (2024, p. 14), in their analysis of 47 studies, concluded:

> The impact of IR [Independent Reading] on attitudes alone provides a compelling reason to incorporate it into reading education. The current findings support the hypothesis that IR satisfies students' curiosity and interests, enriching not only their intellectual but also their emotional lives. Our meta-analysis reinforces the argument that IR should be an essential component of the reading curriculum and a regular practice in reading pedagogy, applicable to both primary and secondary education. However, it is important to remember that IR is not intended to replace teacher-led instruction. Instead, it serves as a complementary activity that enhances students' engagement with reading, making it indispensable not only for supporting reading skill development but also for fostering a love of reading.

Reinforcing these findings, Merke et al. (2024) conducted a meta-analysis of 51 effect studies examining additions to independent reading. These additions included supporting children in selecting appropriate books, implementing strategies to enhance student engagement in reading activities, ensuring accountability for reading volume and content, and increasing opportunities for students to interact about what they read. Their findings demonstrate that such structured approaches contribute significantly to reading proficiency, with particular benefits for students at risk of reading failure.

Given the substantial evidence presented, I argue that providing time for reading for pleasure represents an essential complement to evidence-based reading instruction rather than competing with it. Just as instructional time is dedicated to teaching foundational reading skills, time must also be allocated for children to apply and extend these skills through engagement with self-selected texts. This integration is particularly crucial for children with limited access to books outside school settings. From this perspective, reading for pleasure should be understood not as a practice that competes with instructional priorities but as a vital component of comprehensive literacy education that benefits all children, particularly those from disadvantaged backgrounds. When positioned as complementary rather than competing approaches, both explicit instruction and reading for pleasure can contribute to more equitable literacy outcomes for all children.

Solutions and Best Practice for Addressing Opportunity Inequities

Addressing the opportunity inequities in access to books requires comprehensive, evidence-based strategies that operate at multiple levels—from supporting individual families to implementing systemic policy changes. My fellowship journey revealed several promising approaches that could be implemented or expanded in Australia and other countries to ensure all children have meaningful access to reading materials and opportunities.

Book-Gifting Programmes: Building Home Libraries from Birth

Book-gifting programmes represent one of the most direct and effective approaches to increasing children's access to books from the earliest stages of life. These programmes, which provide free books to children and families, operate in many countries, including Australia, the UK, and the USA, and are usually run by not-for-profit groups that largely rely on philanthropic and government donations or grants.

Research consistently demonstrates the value of these initiatives. Studies by Tura et al. (2023) and Xie et al. (2018) found that sustained book-gifting programmes positively impact parents' reading behaviours and attitudes towards reading with their children, while increasing the frequency of parent-child book sharing and improving children's early literacy skills. Importantly, a UK study by Tura et al. (2023) emphasised that book-gifting schemes need to be long-term in nature to positively influence home literacy environments, highlighting the importance of sustainable funding models.

Dolly Parton's Imagination Library (DPIL) exemplifies the potential impact of well-designed book-gifting programmes. What distinguishes DPIL from many other initiatives is its sustained engagement with families—children are enrolled from birth and receive one book monthly until age five, totalling 60 books during these formative years. During my visit to the Dollywood Foundation in Tennessee, I witnessed the global reach of this programme, which has enrolled over 2.5 million children and distributed more than 210 million books. The DPIL National Impact Report for Australia (United Way Australia, 2023) documents multiple benefits, including increased reading frequency and duration, improved caregiver confidence, and enhanced family engagement with books.

In Australia, there is limited access to DPIL in parts of NSW and Victoria, and there are several other promising book gifting initiatives existing, including Better Beginnings in Western Australia, Raising Literacy Australia, Books in Homes, and the Indigenous Literacy Foundation's Book Supply Programme. These programmes serve different communities and contexts, with some, like the Indigenous Literacy Foundation, ensuring that over 50% of their books feature Indigenous authors and illustrators—simultaneously addressing both access and representation. The economic case for expanding these programmes is compelling. An impact assessment of DPIL Australia suggested the programme can lead to a 14-point increase in Year 3 NAPLAN scores, with an estimated monetary benefit of around $2000 AUD per student (dandolopartners, 2022). This represents a four-to-one return on investment, a conservative estimate that does not account for numerous other educational and social benefits.

Strengthening Library Infrastructure and Creating Reading Opportunities

Evidence consistently demonstrates a strong link between well-resourced school libraries, qualified teacher librarians and improved student literacy outcomes. The annual Australian School Library Survey consistently shows this positive correlation, and international research, such as Lance and Kachel's (2018) review of 34 US statewide studies, has found that students in schools with certified librarians achieve higher standardised test results and are more likely to graduate.

Creating strong reading cultures in schools is equally important. Children need access to diverse, engaging books and opportunities to select and read materials that interest them. By providing authentic choices and dedicated time for reading during the school day, schools can nurture intrinsic motivation and cultivate lifelong reading habits. However, Hendry et al. (2025) highlight that access alone is insufficient when many educators have limited knowledge of children's literature. Their research found that over 37% of pre-service teachers could not name a single author they would recommend to children. This 'professional knowledge gap' limits teachers' ability to make effective recommendations and connect children with texts that might engage them. Promising approaches to addressing this gap include targeted professional development models like Reading for Pleasure Ambassadors programmes and Teacher Reading Groups that build educators' knowledge of diverse, contemporary children's literature within supportive social environments (Hendry et al., 2025).

The solutions highlighted above represent complementary approaches that, when implemented together, can begin to address the complex, multifaceted nature of the opportunity inequity in access to books. By combining early intervention through book gifting, robust school and community library infrastructure, teacher professional knowledge of reading for pleasure, and dedicated time for reading in schools, educational stakeholders and policymakers can collectively ensure all children have the resources and opportunities they need to develop as engaged, enthusiastic readers.

Collaborative Approaches

The Diverse Books for All Coalition

One particularly promising development in addressing both access and representation issues is the formation of the Diverse Books for All Coalition in the USA. While currently limited to the United States with no comparable coalition yet established in Australia or other countries, this coalition brings together over 30 not-for-profit organisations promoting strong foundations for early literacy. As Kyle Zimmer of First Books and the W.K. Kellogg Foundation explained, the coalition addresses three interconnected challenges:

> The lack of access to affordable, quality children's books by and about diverse cultures and races; the need for a clear narrative about the value and benefits of diverse books; and support for parents, caregivers and educators to effectively define, advocate for and integrate diverse books.
>
> (Swartz, 2022)

This collaborative approach recognises that the most effective solutions emerge when organisations with complementary expertise work together towards systemic change. The coalition's focus on both access and representation acknowledges that truly equitable literacy support must ensure children not only have books but also have access to books in which they can see themselves and their communities authentically represented.

Technology-Enhanced Collaborative Models

Another promising collaborative approach is the integration of mobile technology with existing book access initiatives, as exemplified by a recent research initiative, the Kindytxt programme in Western Australia. Designed as a component of the universal Better Beginnings book-gifting programme—a State Library of Western Australia initiative that provides reading resources to all families with newborns and continues to support children's literacy development through to school age—Kindytxt utilised a library-school delivery model to provide 90 text messages over 30 weeks to parents of kindergarten children across all socioeconomic backgrounds. This programme delivered bite-sized literacy activities, contextual information and extension ideas directly to parents' mobile phones, with research showing "similarly high levels of parental support... evident across all socioeconomic strata" (Hill et al., 2024, p. 7). While the Kindytxt initiative has shown promise in research, it has not yet been implemented beyond the original project, highlighting the gap between research evidence and policy implementation. Nevertheless, the model demonstrates how technology could extend the reach of traditional literacy programmes whilst avoiding the stigma sometimes associated with targeted interventions. The cooperative delivery framework enabled schools and libraries to work together to reinforce connections with families, with messages that could be "translated into other languages, saved and shared, thus potentially widening the influence on children's home literacy environments" (Hill et al., 2024, p. 2). Importantly, this approach recognises that addressing opportunity inequities does not require choosing between universal or targeted strategies—the Kindytxt collaborative model allowed universal delivery whilst incorporating differentiated support where needed, with teachers and librarians helping parents adapt activities to suit their child's cultural context and developmental level. This blended approach offers a promising model for leveraging community partnerships and existing infrastructure to improve book access and literacy engagement across diverse communities, though broader implementation will require policy support and funding commitments discussed further in Chapter 9.

Beyond Return on Investment: The Social Justice Imperative

While economic arguments for investing in early literacy access are persuasive—with research suggesting every dollar invested in early years yields two dollars in economic benefit (PwC, 2019)—it is essential to recognise that "children are more than just a return on investment" (Iorio & Yelland, 2021). Thus, providing equitable access to books is fundamentally a social justice issue. Ensuring all children have access to books from an early age, particularly books that reflect their diverse experiences and identities, helps create a more level playing field where all children can contribute to their communities and world. This recognition shifts thinking from viewing book access programmes solely through the lens of educational outcomes or economic returns to understanding them as essential components of a just and equitable society. As Cremin and Scholes (2024) observe in their critical review of the reading for pleasure evidence base, "being a reader in childhood can play a role in reducing educational inequalities. It is not only every child's right, but a matter of social justice that each child is enabled and supported to become a keen and motivated reader" (p. 538).

Connecting Opportunity to the Model for Equitable Literacy Learning Environments

The evidence presented throughout this chapter contributes to the understanding of one of the three essential dimensions of the Model for Equitable Literacy Learning Environments (MELLE) introduced in Chapter 2. Opportunity to read represents a vital component of this model, interconnected with quality instruction and representation in reading materials (Figure 4.1).

Within the MELLE framework, the Opportunity dimension encompasses several critical elements:

- Access to books in the home through initiatives like book-gifting programmes
- Well-resourced school and classroom libraries with qualified librarians
- Dedicated time for reading for pleasure during the school day
- Children's autonomy to select books that interest them
- Equitable access to reading resources including digital resources
- Regular exposure to teacher read-alouds and book sharing

It is recognised within this component of the model that even the highest-quality instruction will have limited impact if children lack access to books and meaningful opportunities to engage with reading. Similarly, diverse representation in reading material (explored in Chapter 5) can only benefit children who have sufficient access to these materials. The opportunity dimension serves as a bridge between quality instruction and

Figure 4.1 Opportunity in the MELLE.

representation, ensuring that children not only learn how to read but also have ample opportunities to practice and develop as engaged, motivated readers. As will be further explored in subsequent chapters, these dimensions function synergistically, with each enhancing the effectiveness of the others when implemented comprehensively.

Conclusion

Throughout this chapter, I have examined the systemic barriers that prevent equitable access to books and reading opportunities for many children, particularly those from economically disadvantaged backgrounds and culturally and racially marginalised communities. This exploration reveals that opportunity inequities are not simply a matter of individual circumstances but also represent an accumulated educational debt that society owes to these communities. The evidence presented demonstrates that without equitable access to books in the home, in schools and in communities, even the highest-quality instruction will have limited impact. For children from marginalised communities, these opportunities serve as pathways to overcome systemic disadvantage and fully participate in literacy practices.

Addressing opportunity disparities requires coordinated action at multiple levels—from family support through book-gifting and early literacy programmes, to school-based initiatives ensuring library resources and reading time, to systemic policy changes that address underlying socioeconomic inequities. While evidence-based reading instruction is essential, it must be complemented by broader opportunities to access and engage with books, supported by educators with strong professional knowledge of children's literature. Such a coordinated approach can create systems where reading engagement becomes possible for every child regardless of socioeconomic background, recognising that educational stakeholders across families, schools, libraries, communities and governmental institutions all have vital roles to play in ensuring equitable literacy opportunities.

Chapter 5 explores the third dimension of the Model for Equitable Literacy Learning Environments: Representation. I will examine how the content and character of the books children read matters profoundly for their engagement, identity development and learning outcomes. The representation dimension intersects with opportunity in critical ways—children need not only access to books, but access to books in which they can see themselves and their communities authentically represented. Through this exploration, I further develop understanding of how these dimensions work together to create truly equitable literacy environments for all children.

References

Adam, H. (2023). *Churchill Fellowship Report: To Enhance Expertise in Children's Books as Vehicles for Disrupting Prejudice and Discrimination.* Churchill Trust. https://www.churchilltrust.com.au/fellow/helen-adam-wa-2022

Adam, H., & Barratt-Pugh, C. (2020). Book sharing with young children: A study of book sharing in four Australian long day care centres. *Journal of Early Childhood Literacy, 23*(3), 348–373. https://doi.org/10.1177/1468798420981745

Adams, R. (2025, 17/04/2025). A third of school staff in England report 'physical underdevelopment' in poor students. *The Guardian.*

Allington, R. L. (2014). How reading volume affects both reading fluency and reading achievement. *International Electronic Journal of Elementary Education, 7*(1), 13–26.

American Library Association. (2022). *School Libraries and Education.* Retrieved 30 August from https://www.ala.org/advocacy/school-libraries

Ball, S. J. (2012). *Global Education Inc: New Policy Networks and the Neo-Liberal Imaginary.* Routledge.

Blair, C., & Raver, C. C. (2016). Poverty, stress, and brain development: New directions for prevention and intervention. *Academic Pediatrics, 16*(3), S30–S36. https://doi.org/10.1016/j.acap.2016.01.010

Boutte, G. S., & Compton-Lilly, C. (2022). Guest editorial: Prioritizing pro-Blackness in literacy research. *Journal of Literacy Research, 54*(3), 323–333.

Braden, E., Boutte, G., Wynter-Hoyte, K., Long, S., Aitken, C., Collins, S., Frazier, J., Gamble, E., Hall, L., Hodge, S., McDonald, C., Merritt, A., Mosso-Taylor, S., Samuel, K., Stout, C., Tafel, J., Warren, T., & Witherspoon, J. (2022). Emancipating early childhood literacy curricula: Pro-Black teaching in K-3 classrooms. *Journal of Early Childhood Literacy, 22*(4), 500–539. https://doi.org/10.1177/14687984221135488

Bus, A. G., Shang, Y., & Roskos, K. (2024). Building a stronger case for independent reading at school. *AERA Open, 10*. https://doi.org/10.1177/23328584241267843

Cassidy, C. (2023, November 27). Australia's poorest children are five years behind richest peers, Naplan analysis shows. *The Guardian*. https://www.theguardian.com/australia-news/2023/nov/27/australias-poorest-children-are-five-years-behind-richest-peers-naplan-analysis-shows

Chamberlain, L., Lacina, J., Bintz, W. P., Jimerson, J. B., Payne, K., & Zingale, R. (2022). Literacy in lockdown: Learning and teaching during COVID-19 school closures. *The Reading Teacher, 75*(5), 557–569. https://doi.org/10.1002/trtr.1961

Children's Defense Fund. (2023). *2023 State of America's Children® Report*. https://www.childrensdefense.org/tools-and-resources/the-state-of-americas-children/

Compton-Lilly, C. (2007). The complexities of reading capital in two Puerto Rican families. *Reading Research Quarterly, 42*(1), 72–98. https://doi.org/10.1598/RRQ.42.1.3

Cormier, C. J. (2023). It's not easy being green: Addressing overrepresentation in special education through culturally responsive pedagogy. *Kappa Delta Pi Record, 58*(1), 10–15.

Cormier, C. J. (2024). Misidentification, misinformation, and miseducation: The experiences of minoritized students and representation in public schools across three societies around the globe. *PJE. Peabody Journal of Education, 99*(1), 1–3. https://doi.org/10.1080/0161956X.2024.2307792

Cremin, T. (2019). *Reading Communities: Why, What and How? Primary Matters*. NATE.

Cremin, T., Mottram, M., Powell, S., Collins, R., & Safford, K. (2014). *Building Communities of Engaged Readers: Reading for Pleasure*. Routledge.

Cremin, T., & Scholes, L. (2024). Reading for pleasure: Scrutinising the evidence base: Benefits, tensions and recommendations. *Language and Education, 38*(4), 537–559. https://doi.org/10.1080/09500782.2024.2324948

dandolopartners (2022). *Dolly Parton's Imagination Library: Impact Assessment*. United Way Australia.

Duke, N. K., Ward, A. E., & Pearson, P. D. (2021). The science of reading comprehension instruction. *The Reading Teacher, 74*(6), 663–672. https://doi.org/10.1002/trtr.1993

Ferguson, D. (2020, February 29). Children are reading less than ever before, research reveals. *The Guardian*. https://www.theguardian.com/education/2020/feb/29/children-reading-less-says-new-research

Fisher, D., & Frey, N. (2018). Raise reading volume through access, choice, discussion, and book talks. *The Reading Teacher*, *72*(1), 89–97. https://doi.org/10.1002/trtr.1691

Gorski, P. C. (2017). *Reaching and Teaching Students in Poverty: Strategies for Erasing the Opportunity Gap* (2nd ed.). Teachers College Press.

Graff, H. J. (1979). *The Literacy Myth: Literacy and Social Structure in the Nineteenth-Century City*. Academic Press.

Graff, H. J. (2010). The literacy myth at thirty. *Journal of Social History*, *43*(3), 635–661. https://doi.org/10.1353/jsh.0.0316

Great School Libraries Campaign. (2023). *Great School Libraries: Equal Futures? An Imbalance of Opportunities*. https://www.greatschoollibraries.org.uk/_files/ugd/8d6dfb_b6f1af1fa9ec48b08b93566dc7608d95.pdf

Grieshaber, S., Shield, P., Luke, A., & Macdonald, S. (2012). Family literacy practices and home literacy resources: An Australian pilot study. *Journal of Early Childhood Literacy*, *12*(2), 113–138. https://doi.org/10.1177/1468798411416888

Hair, N. L., Hanson, J. L., Wolfe, B. L., & Pollak, S. D. (2015). Association of child poverty, brain development, and academic achievement. *JAMA Pediatrics*, *169*(9), 822–829. https://doi.org/10.1001/jamapediatrics.2015.1475

Harms, M. B., & Garrett-Ruffin, S. D. (2023). Disrupting links between poverty, chronic stress, and educational inequality. *NPJ Science of Learning*, *8*(1), 50. https://doi.org/10.1038/s41539-023-00199-2

Heath, S. B. (1983). *Ways with Words: Language, Life, and Work in Communities and Classrooms*. Cambridge University Press.

Hempel-Jorgensen, A., Cremin, T., Harris, D., & Chamberlain, L. (2018). Pedagogy for reading for pleasure in low socio-economic primary schools: Beyond 'pedagogy of poverty?' *Literacy*, *52*(2), 86–94. https://doi.org/10.1111/lit.12157

Hendry, H., Cremin, T., & Harrison, A. (2025). Developing pre-service teachers' pedagogical content knowledge for reading for pleasure: What is missing? What next? *Education Sciences*, *15*(5), 588. https://doi.org/10.3390/educsci15050588

Hill, S. M., Barratt-Pugh, C., Johnson, N. F., & Barblett, L. (2024). Receptiveness of the Kindytxt universal early literacy texting program by parents from low, medium, and high socioeconomic communities. *Early Childhood Education Journal*. https://doi.org/10.1007/s10643-024-01788-5

Iorio, J. M., & Yelland, N. (2021). Children are more than just a return on investment. *Pursuit*. https://pursuit.unimelb.edu.au/articles/children-are-more-than-just-a-return-on-investment

Ladson-Billings, G. (2006). From the achievement gap to the education debt: Understanding achievement in US schools. *Educational Researcher*, *35*(7), 3–12. https://doi.org/10.3102/0013189X035007003

Lance, K. C., & Kachel, D. E. (2018). Why school librarians matter: What years of research tell us. *Phi Delta Kappan*, *99*(7), 15–20. https://doi.org/10.1177/0031721718767854

Lipman, P. (2004). *High Stakes Education: Inequality, Globalization, and Urban School Reform*. Routledge. https://doi.org/10.4324/9780203465509

Lowell, A., Maypilama, E. L., Fasoli, L., Guyula, Y., Yunupiŋu, M., Godwin-Thompson, J., Guyula, A., Yunupiŋu, M., & Armstrong, E. (2018). Building Yolŋu skills, knowledge, and priorities into early childhood assessment and support: Protocol for a qualitative study. *JMIR Research Protocols*, *7*(3), e50. https://doi.org/10.2196/resprot.8722

Merga, M. K. (2019). How do librarians in schools support struggling readers? *English in Education*, *53*(2), 145–160. https://doi.org/10.1080/04250494.2018.1558030

Merke, S., Ganushcak, L., & van Steensel, R. (2024). Effects of additions to independent silent reading on students' reading proficiency, motivation, and behavior: Results of a meta-analysis. *Educational Research Review*, *42*, 100572. https://doi.org/10.1016/j.edurev.2023.100572

New South Wales Department of Education. (2021). *Student Behaviour Strategy 2021*. NSW Department of Education.

Noble, K. G., Houston, S. M., Brito, N. H., Bartsch, H., Kan, E., Kuperman, J. M., Akshoomoff, N., Amaral, D. G., Bloss, C. S., Libiger, O., Schork, N. J., Murray, S. S., Casey, B. J., Chang, L., Ernst, T. M., Frazier, J. A., Gruen, J. R., Kennedy, D. N., Van Zijl, P.,…Sowell, E. R. (2015). Family income, parental education and brain structure in children and adolescents. *Nature Neuroscience*, *18*(5), 773–778. https://doi.org/10.1038/nn.3983

Poverty & Inequality. (2024). *Poverty in Australia: A Snapshot* https://povertyandinequality.acoss.org.au/wp-content/uploads/2024/09/poverty-in-australia-a-snapshot.pdf

PwC. (2019). *A Smart Investment for a Smarter Australia: Economic Analysis of Universal Early Childhood Education in the Year Before School in Australia*. The Front Project.

Rennie, J. (2016). Confessions from a reading program: Building connections, competence and confidence. In J. Rennie & H. Harper (Eds.), *Literacy Education and Indigenous Australians: Theory, Research and Practice* (pp. 87–108). Springer. https://doi.org/10.1007/978-981-13-8629-9_6

Rudolph, S. (2019). *Unsettling the Gap: Race, Politics and Indigenous Education*. Peter Lang.

Sanders, C. K., & Scanlon, E. (2021). The digital divide is a human rights issue: Advancing social inclusion through social work advocacy. *Journal of Human Rights and Social Work*, *6*(2), 130–143. https://doi.org/10.1007/s41134-020-00147-9

Scholastic. (2019). *Kids and Family Reading Report, 7th Edition: Finding Their Story*. Scholastic Inc.

Scholastic. (2024). *Kids and Family Reading Report* (8th ed.). Scholastic Inc.

Shanahan, T. (2020). Limiting children to books they can already read: Why it reduces their opportunity to learn. *American Educator, 44*(2), 13–17.

Shanahan, T. (2024). Isn't independent reading a research based practice? *Shanahan on Literacy.* https://www.shanahanonliteracy.com/blog/isnt-independent-reading-a-research-based-practice

Shirodkar, S. (2019). Bias against indigenous Australians: Implicit association test results for Australia. *Journal of Australian Indigenous Issues, 22*(3–4), 3–34.

Softlink Education. (2024). *Australian School Library Survey Report 2023*.

Stanovich, K. E. (1986). Matthew effects in reading: Some consequences of individual differences in the acquisition of literacy. *Reading Research Quarterly, 21*(4), 360–407. https://doi.org/10.1598/RRQ.21.4.1

Street, B. V. (1984). *Literacy in Theory and Practice*. Cambridge University Press.

Sun, Y.-J., Sahakian, B. J., Langley, C., Yang, A., Jiang, Y., Kang, J., Zhao, X., Li, C., Cheng, W., & Feng, J. (2023). Early-initiated childhood reading for pleasure: Associations with better cognitive performance, mental well-being and brain structure in young adolescence. *Psychological Medicine, 54*(2), 359–373. https://doi.org/10.1017/S0033291723001381

Swartz, M (2022, December 8). A new collation promotes children's self-esteem (and expanded worldviews) through diverse books. *Best Practices*.

Thomas, J., McCosker, A., Parkinson, S., Hegarty, K., Featherstone, D., Kennedy, J., Holcombe-James, I., Ormond-Parker, L., & Ganley, L. (2023). *Measuring Australia's digital Divide: Australian Digital Inclusion Index: 2023*. ARC Centre of Excellence for Automated Decision-Making and Society, RMIT University, Swinburne University of Technology, and Telstra. https://doi.org/10.25916/528s-ny91

Tura, F., Wood, C., Thompson, R., & Lushey, C. (2023). Evaluating the impact of book gifting on the reading behaviours of parents and young children. *Early Years, 43*(1), 75–90. https://doi.org/10.1080/09575146.2021.1908234

United Way Australia. (2023). *Dolly Parton's Imagination Library National Impact Report 2021–2023*. United Way Australia.

Weinstein, D., Jung, K., Jauriqui, V., & Rosenthal, E. L. (2020). *Rags-to-Riches, Welfare Queens and Broken Families: Media Representations of Poverty and their Impact on Audiences*. USC Annenberg: Norman Lear Center.

Xie, Q. W., Chan, C. H. Y., Ji, Q., & Chan, C. L. W. (2018). Psychosocial effects of parent-child book reading interventions: A meta-analysis. *Pediatrics, 141*(4), e20172675. https://doi.org/10.1542/peds.2017-2675

Representation in Reading Materials 5

Introduction: Representation as a Foundation for Equitable Reading Instruction

Having established the theoretical foundations for equitable literacy education in Chapters 1 and 2, examined quality instruction (Chapter 3), and explored opportunity disparities (Chapter 4), this chapter turns to the third essential dimension of the Model for Equitable Literacy Environments (MELLE): representation in reading materials and educator practice. This element is not merely complementary to effective instruction and opportunity to read—it forms a critical foundation for truly inclusive literacy environments where all children can thrive. As illustrated in the model presented in Chapter 2, representation interacts dynamically with both quality instruction and opportunity. Even the most evidence-based instructional practices may fail to engage children who cannot see themselves reflected in the texts they encounter. Similarly, providing ample opportunities to read has limited impact when available books present a narrow, homogeneous view of the world that excludes many children's lived experiences. Representation, therefore, is not an optional enhancement but a fundamental requirement for equitable literacy education.

If children do not feel visible and recognised as equal members of the classroom, it is little wonder when their learning journey, motivation and outcomes suffer. Once a child begins formal schooling, or even earlier through early education and care, they spend most of their waking hours in an educational environment. It is imperative, therefore, that these environments are welcoming spaces for all children where they feel they belong as

DOI: 10.4324/9781003628217-5

equal members of the wider group. This is where the matter of representation is vital: Representation in books and other learning materials, and representation in teaching and classroom pedagogy, processes and practices. Thus, as part of investigating ways to improve reading outcomes, children's motivation to read should not be overlooked. Research in the USA consistently shows that African American boys have the lowest reading achievement and are less likely to be interested in reading (Husband, 2012; Tatum et al., 2021). Similarly, in Australia, literacy rates among Aboriginal children, particularly those in remote areas, are consistently behind those of their non-Indigenous counterparts (National Indigenous Australians Agency, 2024). While the factors behind these outcomes are complex, one thing that is constantly overlooked is the question of what children are expected to read. Why are children from Indigenous and CARM backgrounds expected to develop reading skills and a love of reading when they are taught to read, and expected to read, with materials that represent lives unlike their own and which often position their lives as background, strange or invisible? Is it any wonder that it is often children from Indigenous and CARM backgrounds who are the most reluctant readers?

Many of the diverse scholars I met with during my Churchill Fellowship expressed frustration that this aspect is ignored or overlooked in the quest to improve literacy outcomes. This sentiment was echoed by educators and researchers across both the United States and United Kingdom during my fellowship and is especially concerning when a strong body of evidence shows the difference that can be made to children's learning outcomes through the provision of books reflecting children's lives, experiences and backgrounds. In this chapter, I examine how representation in reading materials intersects with both quality instruction and opportunity to read (as explored in Chapters 3 and 4), demonstrating that these three dimensions must work collectively to create truly equitable literacy environments. While previous chapters have highlighted how inequitable access to quality instruction and reading opportunities disproportionately affects children from marginalised backgrounds, this chapter will illustrate how the persistent lack of diverse representation compounds these inequities, creating additional barriers to literacy development for many children.

The Lack of Diverse Books in Education Settings

Representation in children's literature is a critical issue that directly impacts children's engagement with reading, their sense of identity, and their understanding of the world around them. Despite increasing awareness of its importance, research conducted over the last two decades consistently shows the world presented in children's books is overwhelmingly white, male, and middle class (Adam, 2019; Adam et al., 2019; Adam & Urquhart, 2023; Boutte et al., 2008; Caple & Tian, 2021; Crisp et al., 2016). The implications of this lack of diversity are far-reaching, as children from underrepresented backgrounds rarely see themselves reflected in the books they encounter in educational settings, making it difficult for them to connect with literature that does not reflect their lived experiences, cultural identities, or family structures—with significant consequences for their educational and social development. My doctoral studies in early learning centres in Australia found that only 18% of a total 2314 books in the book collections of participating centres portrayed any racial diversity; furthermore, in the majority of those, the representation was outdated, stereotypical, or characters were simply presented as background characters to white main protagonists (Adam, 2019). More alarmingly, less than 1% of books available to children in my studies showed authentic representation of Aboriginal and Torres Strait Islander people (Adam & Barratt-Pugh, 2020). Given the cultural diversity of Australian society and the significance of Indigenous heritage to national identity, these findings are particularly troubling.

Recent analyses of award-listed Australian children's picture books reveal that while diverse characters are becoming more prevalent in contemporary publications, they often appear as non-specific background characters rather than central protagonists (Adam & Urquhart, 2023; Caple & Tian, 2021)—reflecting what Bishop (1990) termed 'token' inclusion. Compounding this problem, a large-scale 2022 Victoria University study confirmed a "severe under-representation of First Nations writers and Writers of Colour within Australian literature" (Atkinson, 2022), diminishing authentic cultural representation. Similar patterns exist internationally: the London-based Centre for Literacy in Primary Education (CLPE) "Reflecting Realities" research shows UK books featuring minority ethnic characters increased from 4% (2017) to 30% (2022) before declining to 17% (2023), while the Wisconsin-based Cooperative Children's Book Center (2023) longitudinal tracking in the US reported that despite 51% of books containing Black, Indigenous, People of Color (BIPOC) content in 2024, those featuring BIPOC primary characters decreased from 40% to 37% between 2023 and 2024. While these trends show some progress, they remain far from proportionate representation, and recent declines raise concerns about sustainability.

Adding to these issues is a significant backlash against diverse books, leading to an alarming rise in book bans and censorship, particularly in the USA (Friedman, 2022; Zalusky, 2023). Alarmingly, in the 2023–2024 school year, there were over 10,000 instances of book bans in USA public schools relating to 4218 unique book titles. Some 36% of these featured characters of colour and 25% LGBTQIA+ characters. With over 50% of children in the US being children of colour, "this erasure in school libraries has deeply harmful impacts on the mental health of students of color" (PEN America, 2024). Such bans continue to increase under the current US presidential administration and are increasingly being signed into law governing schools, school libraries and even public libraries across the nation (American Library Association, 2023). The impact of these book bans means that while publication of diverse books may be on the rise, their availability for children at school is under increasing threat. Albeit to a lesser extent, calls for book bans and restrictions are also on the rise in the UK and in Australia (Karvelas, 2024; Leggatt, 2022).

Thus, consistent lack of diverse books across education contexts represents what can only be described as an educational and equity crisis. With a strong body of evidence demonstrating the impact diverse books can have on children from underrepresented backgrounds and their educational and social-emotional outcomes, as well as the value for all children through the disruption of prejudice and discrimination, this situation demands urgent attention and action.

The Impact of Representation on Cognitive and Socioemotional Development

For children to succeed in their learning, they need to feel a sense of belonging and inclusion in the classroom. Learning environments that reflect, connect with, and build on children's diverse identities and funds of knowledge (Morrison et al., 2019; O'Keeffe et al., 2018) can make a powerful difference to children's sense of belonging and ultimately to their educational and life outcomes.

Mirrors, Windows and Sliding Glass Doors

Beyond academic outcomes, representation plays a vital role in children's socioemotional development, with early childhood being particularly significant for forming attitudes about oneself and others (Australian Government Department of Education, 2022). Rudine Sims Bishop's (1990) groundbreaking metaphor of "mirrors, windows, and sliding glass doors" provides a powerful framework for understanding literature's multiple functions in children's lives:

> Books are sometimes windows, offering views of worlds that may be real or imagined, familiar or strange. These windows are also sliding glass doors, and readers have only to walk through in imagination to become part of whatever world has been created or recreated by the author. When lighting conditions are just right, however, a window can also be a mirror. Literature transforms human experience and reflects it back to us, and in that reflection we can see our own lives and experiences as part of the larger human experience. Reading, then, becomes a means of self-affirmation, and readers often seek their mirrors in books.
> (Bishop, 1990, p. ix)

Since Bishop's foundational work, researchers have consistently demonstrated the importance of providing children with both mirrors that reflect their own experiences and windows that offer perspectives on others' lives (Tschida et al., 2014). This dual function develops cross-cultural understanding (Adam et al., 2023; Harper & Brand, 2010; Magos, 2018) and facilitates children's ability to "make connections, form relationships and create community with others". (Short, 2012, p. 9)

Children develop their sense of identity and perceptions of others remarkably early—as young as three months old (Bar-Haim et al., 2006; Sangrigoli & De Schonen, 2004), making them particularly vulnerable to messages conveyed through books and media (Adam and Barratt-Pugh, 2020). When children rarely see themselves represented, they may internalise negative messages about their relevance, affecting identity formation and self-esteem; conversely, authentic representations validate their identities and affirm their place in society. For all children, diverse books foster empathy and cross-cultural understanding (Bennett et al., 2018), while for those from underrepresented groups, they develop a crucial sense of belonging—a critical prerequisite for engagement and motivation. Kidd and Castano's (2013) research demonstrates that exposure to diverse perspectives through literature develops children's capacity for understanding different worldviews and shapes their identity development. Without such exposure, children from non-dominant cultures often experience 'othering' or exclusion, where difference is positioned as aberrant rather than valued (Plastow & Hillel, 2010)—contributing to negative educational experiences for many Indigenous and culturally diverse children (Cormier, 2024; Berry, 2024; Jackson-Barrett, 2021).

The Impact of Representation on Academic Outcomes

The cognitive benefits of diverse representation in children's literature are substantial and well-documented. When children encounter books that reflect their lived experiences and cultural backgrounds, they engage more deeply with texts on multiple cognitive levels (Boutte et al., 2008; Souto-Manning et al., 2018a). Evans' (2010) study examining the impact of culturally relevant literature in elementary classrooms found that children demonstrated increased participation in classroom discussions, improved comprehension, and enhanced writing skills when engaging with texts that reflected their cultural backgrounds. Their comprehension improves as they more readily draw upon background knowledge and cultural schemas to make inferences and connections, while vocabulary acquisition is enhanced when new words connect to existing knowledge frameworks. Furthermore, diverse literature fosters critical thinking by encouraging children to consider multiple perspectives and engage with complex social issues.

This evidence demonstrates how diverse representation enables children to engage as readers through the four roles of the reader identified by Freebody and Luke (1990) and central to the Quality Instruction dimension of the MELLE, as discussed in Chapter 3. When children engage with diverse texts, they strengthen their capabilities as code-breakers by connecting decoding skills to meaningful, culturally relevant content. As text participants, they draw on cultural schemas and lived experiences to make deeper connections with texts that reflect their backgrounds (Luke & Freebody, 1999). Diverse literature particularly enriches the text user and text analyst roles by providing authentic contexts for critical literacy development, enabling children to question representations, consider multiple perspectives and recognise how texts position readers (Freebody & Luke, 1990; Luke & Freebody, 1999).

This integration complements Duke and Cartwright's (2021) Active View of Reading, which emphasises that reading involves cognitive, ecological and psychological dimensions working in concert. Culturally relevant texts strengthen the bridging processes between word recognition and language comprehension while positively impacting the reader's self-concept, motivation and identity—psychological factors central to reading success. When children see themselves represented in what they read, these dimensions are mutually reinforced, creating 'virtuous cycles' of reading development where engagement leads to practice, improved skills and enhanced motivation. For children from underrepresented groups, seeing themselves in texts validates their identities and cultural knowledge, enabling more confident engagement as text users in various social contexts.

Building on these understandings of why representation matters, recent empirical evidence from intervention studies demonstrates the measurable impact of diverse books on children's educational outcomes and socioemotional development. The First Book Research & Insights study, *The impact of a diverse classroom library* (2023), provides particularly compelling evidence of the academic impact of diverse representation. This five-month study tracked the effects of adding diverse books to classroom libraries across the United States and found:

- Student reading assessment scores increased by an average of 9 points, which was 3 points higher than nationally expected average yearly gains
- Specifically, LGBTQ+ books improved scores by 4.5 points on average, while bilingual books yielded a 7-point improvement
- The lowest-scoring students showed the greatest improvements, with gains of 11 points on average
- Classrooms serving younger children (ages 4–6) showed particularly impressive gains of 13 points on average
- Student reading time increased by 4 hours per week on average

These findings demonstrate that the impact of diverse representation can be observed within a relatively short timeframe—five months in this case—and that the benefits are particularly significant for students who may be struggling with reading. This provides compelling evidence that addressing representation is not merely a matter of inclusivity for its own sake, but an evidence-based approach to enhancing literacy outcomes for all children—directly connecting to the evidence-based practice emphasis discussed in Chapter 3 while addressing the opportunity gaps highlighted in Chapter 4. Therefore, providing children with books that authentically reflect diversity should be considered essential in educational environments. When children cannot see themselves represented or see only stereotypical representations their sense of belonging and ability to participate fully in learning experiences are compromised. As Tatum states, "Neither effective reading strategies nor comprehensive literacy reform efforts will close the achievement gap in a race- and class-based society unless meaningful texts are at the core of the curriculum" (2015, p. 2).

Culturally Responsive Pedagogy When Using Diverse Books

While the availability of diverse books is essential, how educators engage children with these books is equally important. Simply providing diverse books without critical engagement fails to realise their transformative potential. A culturally responsive approach to literacy offers a powerful framework to maximise the impact of diverse representation. Culturally responsive pedagogy emphasises the importance of leveraging students' cultural knowledge as assets rather than deficits (Souto-Manning et al., 2018a). "Culturally responsive pedagogies as those that 'actively value, and mobilise as resources, the cultural repertoires and intelligences that students bring to the learning relationship'" (Morrison et al., 2019 p. 59). This approach recognises that effective literacy instruction must build upon, rather than suppress or ignore, children's cultural knowledge and experiences.

Critical literacy, a complementary approach, involves reading that goes beyond conventional notions of comprehension to engage with issues of power, equity and social justice. Such practice enables students to engage with texts in ways that help them understand and confront social, political or economic realities (Boutte et al., 2011; Souto-Manning et al., 2018a). When applied to the use of diverse books, critical literacy practices empower children to:

1. Question whose voices are heard and whose are missing in texts
2. Examine how different cultural groups are portrayed
3. Connect texts to their own lives and broader social contexts
4. Recognise and challenge stereotypes and biases
5. Consider multiple perspectives and interpretations

Research conducted with elementary students has demonstrated how critical literacy discussions coupled with diverse books led to measurable changes in students' perspectives towards diversity. Through interactive read-alouds and guided discussions, students developed not only greater awareness of cultural differences but also deeper empathy and commitment to tolerance (Evans, 2010; Souto-Manning & Martell, 2016). In practice, culturally responsive engagement with diverse books involves:

Creating Dialogic Spaces: Creating environments where students can engage in authentic dialogue about texts through 'turn and talk' opportunities, whole-group discussions and written reflections that encourage children to articulate their understanding of diversity (Souto-Manning et al., 2018b).

Critical Questioning: Guiding students in questioning texts by asking who is represented, whose perspectives are centred or marginalised, and how power relationships are portrayed. This helps children develop critical consciousness about representation in literature and media (Boutte et al., 2011).

Connecting to Lived Experiences: Encouraging children to make connections between texts and their own lives, validating their cultural knowledge and experiences as resources for learning (Morrison et al., 2019).

Moving Beyond Awareness to Action: Engaging children in using their literacy skills to address issues of equity and justice in their communities, making literacy learning meaningful and empowering (Souto-Manning & Martell, 2016).

Implementation Through Professional Learning

While the evidence for the benefits of diverse libraries is robust, implementation often presents significant challenges. The First Book study found that while 99% of educators believed having a diverse classroom library was important, and 58% believed their current library adequately reflected their students' identities, diverse titles comprised only 28% of their libraries. This gap between perception and reality highlights the need for structured frameworks and professional learning to help educators critically evaluate their book collections.

In my research exploring educators' experiences implementing diverse book collections (Adam, 2019; Adam and Barratt-Pugh, 2020; Adam, 2021; Adam & Byrne, 2023), several common barriers emerged:

1. **Limited availability of high-quality diverse books**: Many educators struggled to locate books that authentically represented diverse experiences, particularly for specific cultural groups.
2. **Insufficient knowledge for selection**: Educators often lacked confidence in, and knowledge for, evaluating the nature and quality of representation in books.
3. **Lack of cultural knowledge and competence**: Some educators avoided addressing diversity and diverse cultures due to their own acknowledged lack of knowledge and confidence. Conversely, for some others, failing to recognise their own limited knowledge resulted in a false confidence whereby they focused on tokenistic representation often using books focused only on festivals and outdated or inaccurate representation of diverse groups.
4. **Integration beyond 'special' times**: Educators found it challenging to integrate diverse books throughout the curriculum, tending to only use them during cultural celebrations or designated diversity units.

5. **Concerns about discussing sensitive topics**: Some educators expressed hesitation about engaging with books that addressed issues of racism, discrimination or cultural differences.

The implementation of culturally responsive pedagogy with diverse books requires intentional professional learning for educators, including in Initial Teacher Education. This involves developing skills in selecting authentic diverse literature, facilitating critical discussions, and creating classroom environments where all students feel safe to share their perspectives and experiences. To address implementation challenges, successful interventions have strategically paired diverse book selection and provision with comprehensive professional development opportunities.

A recent impact study examining my research and professional learning with pre-service and practising educators over ten years in Australia demonstrates significant benefits of training in culturally responsive use of diverse literature (Enriquez Watt & Adam, 2023). The research reveals a multilayered impact: educators incorporated recommendations on selecting and using diverse books into their daily practice, implementing inclusive teaching strategies and critically examining their assumptions about culturally diverse students; children demonstrated enhanced enjoyment during book sharing, strengthened sense of belonging, and decreased instances of bullying behaviour; and school leaders reported broader community benefits, with school environments becoming more inclusive, demonstrating greater respect for diversity, and fostering a stronger collective sense of belonging. Particularly noteworthy was that parents from diverse backgrounds expressed feeling more included and valued opportunities to share books in their own languages with their children's classes or school libraries. Participants in the impact study emphasised that this work has the potential to initiate new conversations and challenge established cultural paradigms, ultimately transforming the lives of children, educators and communities—highlighting the wider societal relevance of this research beyond merely academic outcomes.

The MELLE presented in this book is intended to support educators in the implementation of culturally responsive literacy education. As one principal noted following a presentation on the MELLE:

> Dr Adam's work highlighting the lack of cultural inclusivity reflected in children's literature has had a transformative effect on how our school plans, implements and assesses reading instruction...We are now not only working with the wider school community to make sure parents and carers are aware of the importance of working with their

children to select a diverse range of reading material but also encouraging parents and carers to look critically at home reading libraries to ensure they reflect diversity. This process has generated significant conversations amongst the parent group and enabled an ongoing connection between school and home.

(Boylan, 2025, personal communication)

This evidence illustrates how culturally responsive implementation of diverse books can extend beyond the classroom to influence entire school communities, creating more inclusive environments where all families feel welcomed and valued.

Reimagining Curricula with Representation at the Core

The evidence presented in this chapter makes a compelling case for reimagining educational curricula with representation at the core. This involves moving beyond occasional or supplementary inclusion of diverse texts to embedding authentic representation throughout the curriculum. Such an approach requires systematic attention to both the content of curricula and the pedagogical practices that support meaningful engagement with diverse literature.

Effective evaluation of diverse materials should consider:

1. **Authenticity and accuracy**: Materials should present authentic representations of cultures, avoiding stereotypes and oversimplifications. This often involves considering the author's background, research, and consultation with cultural insiders.
2. **Currency and specificity**: Generic or dated representations of cultures should be avoided in favour of specific, contemporary portrayals that acknowledge the diversity within cultural groups.
3. **Balance of universal and culture-specific themes**: Effective diverse texts often balance universal themes that all children can relate to with specific cultural elements that provide windows into different experiences.
4. **Representation across genres and formats**: Diverse representation should span all literary genres and formats, including fiction, non-fiction, poetry, and digital texts, rather than being confined to specific categories like folktales or historical narratives.
5. **Positive and realistic portrayals**: Materials should present positive and realistic portrayals that recognise resilient, thriving cultures and communities, and avoid negative and stereotypical representations of struggle and adversity.

Thus, to effectively implement the principles discussed in this chapter, educators need practical tools to assess their current collections. Based on the research presented, Table 5.1 presents an assessment framework that can help educators evaluate representation in their book collections. This framework provides educators with a starting point for assessing and improving representation in their book collections. By systematically examining these dimensions, teachers can identify gaps and strengths in their current resources and develop targeted plans for enhancement.

Beyond quantifying representation, educators need tools to evaluate the quality and nature of cultural representation in books. Extending on Bishop's (1992) foundational work, I developed a Cultural Diversity Categories Framework (Table 5.2) for my doctoral research which helps educators distinguish between different types of cultural representation. This framework can help educators move beyond simply counting diverse books to critically evaluating how cultures are portrayed. When used alongside the Representation Audit Framework (Table 5.1), it enables a more nuanced assessment of classroom libraries and can guide more informed selection of diverse literature.

Embedding Diverse Literature Across the Curriculum

Meaningful integration of diverse literature extends beyond building a collection to embedding these texts across the curriculum. To this end, I recommend a culturally responsive curriculum mapping approach that identifies opportunities to incorporate diverse perspectives across subject areas and throughout the academic year, rather than relegating cultural diversity to designated heritage months or special units.

In practice, this means situating diverse texts as central rather than peripheral to the curriculum, positioning them as core materials rather than supplementary or optional additions. It involves using diverse literature to support learning across all subject areas, including mathematics, science, social studies and the arts, recognising that cultural perspectives enrich understanding in every discipline. Crucially, this approach ensures diverse perspectives are represented throughout the academic year, not just during cultural celebrations or commemorative periods. Rather than isolating cultural diversity as a separate topic, curriculum can be organised around substantive concepts and enduring understandings that authentically incorporate multiple cultural perspectives, histories and knowledge systems as integral to learning rather than as occasional additions.

Table 5.1 Representation Audit Framework for Classroom Libraries

Assessment Area	Questions to Consider	Action Steps
Quantity	What percentage of books feature protagonists from diverse backgrounds? How does this compare to your classroom/community demographics?	Aim for representation that reflects the diversity of your classroom and the broader society.
Quality	Are diverse characters presented authentically, avoiding stereotypes? Are they central to the narrative rather than peripheral?	Ensure multiple authentic portrayals by diverse authors. Avoid books with stereotypical or tokenistic representations—if used ensure this is in a critical way to evaluate stereotypes and misconceptions.
Currency	When were the books published? Do they present contemporary as well as historical perspectives?	Ensure your collection includes contemporary portrayals of diverse groups alongside historically important works.
Genre Balance	Are diverse characters represented across all genres?	Intentionally seek diverse representation across different genres, including poetry fantasy, science fiction, and realistic fiction.
Creator Diversity	What proportion of books are written/illustrated by creators from the backgrounds portrayed?	Increase the proportion of books created by diverse authors/illustrators, particularly for books depicting specific cultural experiences.
Usage Patterns	How often are diverse books used in instruction compared to other books?	Track book usage and ensure diverse books are integrated throughout the curriculum and academic year.

Table 5.2 Cultural Diversity Categories Framework

Categories	Indicators
Culturally Authentic/ Specific/ Conscious	• "illuminate the experience of growing up a member of a particular, non-white cultural group" (Bishop, 1992) • Have potential to increase appreciation and understandings of those not from this culture • Books are written by people of the culture reflected in the book* • "Written with a primary goal of speaking to and representing the experiences of underrepresented/ marginalized groups" (Crisp et al., 2016 p. 34)
Culturally Generic/ Socially Conscious	• "featuring characters who are members of so-called minority groups, but contain few, if any specific details that might serve to define those characters culturally." (Bishop, 1992) • Assumed audience is White • Themes often present White European/American/Australian values and activities • Characters may be portrayed in stereotypical ways in illustrations. • "Written with a social agenda, intended to promote acceptance and harmony, or at least tolerance of different groups" (Crisp et al., 2016 p. 34)
Culturally Neutral/ Melting Pot	• "feature people of colour but are fundamentally about something else" (Bishop, 1992) • "cultural authenticity is not likely to be a major consideration" (Bishop, 1992) • The character/s of "colour" could be replaced with a white character with no impact on the overall story • "presenting a colour-blind view of the world and/or depicting people across the rainbow of cultural identities without acknowledging it explicitly" (Crisp et al., 2016 p. 34)

* Some books have been written as a collaboration between an author and members of an underrepresented group. Such books usually contain an endorsement or a statement of permission or collaboration from the member/s of the underrepresented group.

Note: In nonfiction/informational texts rather than look at "characters" look at the representation of people.

As noted by one principal:

> Dr Adam's work has led us to review every aspect of our approach to reading, including the representation of our reading resources and classroom instruction. Her practical evidence-based approach has enabled staff to collaboratively reflect on best practice and restructure their reading planning...her work is having an ongoing positive effect on our policy and programs in all areas of the curriculum, including the resources we choose to use in areas such as History, Science and Health...Prior to working with Dr Adam, we were oblivious to the impact and importance of selecting reading resources that reflect culturally diverse literature to support principles of diversity.
> (Boylan, 2025, personal communication)

This illustrates how representation can extend beyond literacy instruction to inform curriculum development across all subject areas, creating a more holistic approach to diversity and inclusion.

Connecting Representation to the Model for Equitable Literacy Environments

The evidence presented throughout this chapter demonstrates how representation in reading materials forms one of the three essential dimensions of the MELLE first introduced in Chapter 2. This dimension functions in dynamic interaction with quality instruction (Chapter 3) and opportunity to read (Chapter 4) to create truly equitable literacy environments (Figure 5.1).

Within the MELLE framework, the Representation dimension encompasses several critical elements:

- Authentic portrayal of diverse identities, experiences and perspectives in multiple texts
- Critical examination of how power and privilege operate in texts
- Challenging dominant narratives and stereotypes
- Affirming the identities and experiences of marginalised students
- Providing both mirrors in which children see themselves and windows into others' experiences
- Ensuring representation across multiple genres, formats and perspectives
- Culturally Responsive Pedagogy as foundation to practice

80 Creating Equitable Literacy Learning Environments

Figure 5.1 Representation in the MELLE.

This dimension of the model recognises that even with quality instruction and ample opportunity to read, children's literacy development is compromised when they cannot see themselves or their communities authentically represented in the texts they encounter. As Bishop's (1990) mirrors, windows and sliding glass doors metaphor illustrates, representation serves multiple essential functions in literacy development—validating children's identities, broadening their perspectives, and inviting them to step into different worlds and experiences.

The representation dimension completes the triad of essential elements in equitable literacy environments. While quality instruction provides the pedagogical foundation and opportunity ensures access to reading materials and experiences, representation determines whether those materials and experiences will meaningfully engage and affirm all children as literacy learners.

Conclusion

The evidence presented throughout this chapter demonstrates that representation in reading materials is not an optional enhancement but an essential component of equitable literacy education. The persistent lack of diverse representation in children's literature, documented by research across Australia, the United States and the United Kingdom, represents an educational inequity that disproportionately affects children from underrepresented backgrounds. Despite the clear evidence for the importance of representation, there remains a substantial gap between the diversity of society and the representation found in children's literature—a gap particularly pronounced in educational settings, where the books available to children often present a narrow and unrepresentative view of the world. Addressing this disparity requires concerted effort at multiple levels, from individual educators selecting more diverse texts to systemic changes in publishing, curriculum development and educational policy.

Moving from this discussion of representation, Chapter 6 will examine how diverse children's literature can be used specifically to disrupt prejudice and discrimination, building on the foundation established here to explore how educators can move beyond representation to active anti-bias education. Chapter 7 will further explore how the three dimensions of the MELLE—quality instruction, opportunity and representation—intersect and reinforce each other to create comprehensive literacy environments where all children can thrive. By understanding these intersections, educators can develop more integrated approaches that address all aspects of equitable literacy education simultaneously. By integrating representation with quality instruction and reading opportunity, and by explicitly addressing prejudice and discrimination, the Model for Equitable Literacy Learning Environments offers a comprehensive approach to literacy education that can help create truly inclusive learning environments where all children thrive as readers and as members of diverse communities.

References

Adam, H. (2019). *Cultural diversity and children's literature: Kindergarten educators' practices to support principles of cultural diversity through book sharing* [Doctoral dissertation, Edith Cowan University].

Adam, H. (2021). When authenticity goes missing: How monocultural children's literature is silencing the voices and contributing to invisibility of children from minority backgrounds. *Education Sciences, 11*(1), 32. https://doi.org/10.3390/educsci11010032

Adam, H., Barblett, L., Kirk, G., & Boutte, G. S. (2023). (Re)considering equity, inclusion and belonging in the updating of the Early Years Learning Framework for Australia: The potential and pitfalls of book sharing. *Contemporary Issues in Early Childhood, 24*(2), 189–207. https://doi.org/10.1177/14639491231176897

Adam, H., & Barratt-Pugh, C. (2020). The challenge of monoculturalism: What books are educators sharing with children and what messages do they send? *The Australian Educational Researcher*, 47(4), 815–836. https://doi.org/10.1007/s13384-019-00375-7

Adam, H., Barratt-Pugh, C., & Haig, Y. (2019). "Portray cultures other than ours": How children's literature is being used to support the diversity goals of the Australian Early Years Learning Framework. *The Australian Educational Researcher*, 46(3), 549–563. https://doi.org/10.1007/s13384-019-00302-w

Adam, H., & Byrne, M. (2023). 'I'm not from a country, I'm from Australia' Costumes, scarves, and fruit on their heads: The urgent need for Culturally Responsive Pedagogy when sharing diverse books with children. *The Australian Educational Researcher*, 51(4), 1121–1140. https://doi.org/10.1007/s13384-023-00631-x

Adam, H., & Urquhart, Y. (2023). A cause for hope or an unwitting complicity? The representation of cultural diversity in award-listed children's picturebooks in Australia. *Bookbird: A Journal of International Children's Literature*, 61(2), 48–58. https://doi.org/10.1353/bkb.2023.0023

American Library Association. (2023). *Adverse Legislation in the States*. https://www.ala.org/advocacy/adverse-legislation-states

Atkinson, F. (2022). Research confirms lack of cultural diversity in published literature. Victoria University. https://www.vu.edu.au/about-vu/news-events/news/research-confirms-lack-of-cultural-diversity-in-published-literature

Australian Government Department of Education. (2022). *Belonging, Being & Becoming: The Early Years Learning Framework for Australia V2.0*. Commonwealth of Australia.

Australian Government National Indigenous Australians Agency (2024). *Aboriginal and Torres Strait Islander Health Performance Framework: 2.04 Literacy and Numeracy*. Australian Institute and Health and Welfare.

Bar-Haim, Y., Ziv, T., Lamy, D., & Hodes, R. M. (2006). Nature and nurture in own-race face processing. *Psychological Science*, 17(2), 159–163. https://doi.org/10.1111/j.1467-9280.2006.01679.x

Bennett, S. V., Gunn, A. A., Gayle-Evans, G., Barrera, E. S., & Leung, C. B. (2018). Culturally responsive literacy practices in an early childhood community. *Early Childhood Education Journal*, 46(2), 241–248. https://doi.org/10.1007/s10643-017-0839-9

Berry, F. (2024). Race education: Why does it matter and how should educators go about it? *Support for Learning*, 40(2), 112–220. https://doi.org/10.1111/1467-9604.12492

Bishop, R. (1992). Multicultural literature for children: Making informed choices. In V. Harris (Ed.), *Teaching Multicultural Literature in Grades K-8* (pp. 37–53). Christopher-Gordon.

Bishop, R. S. (1990). Mirrors, windows, and sliding glass doors. *Perspectives: Choosing and Using Books for the Classroom, 6*(3), ix–xi.

Boutte, G. S., Hopkins, R., & Waklatsi, T. (2008). Perspectives, voices, and worldviews in frequently read children's books. *Early Education and Development, 19*(6), 941–962. https://doi.org/10.1080/10409280802206643

Boutte, G. S., Lopez-Robertson, J., & Powers-Costello, E. (2011). Moving beyond colorblindness in early childhood classrooms. *Early Childhood Education Journal, 39*(5), 335–342. https://doi.org/10.1007/s10643-011-0457-x

Caple, H., & Tian, P. (2021). I see you: Do you see me? Investigating the representation of diversity in prize winning Australian early childhood picture books. *Australian Educational Researcher, 49*, 175–191. https://doi.org/10.1007/s13384-020-00423-7

Centre for Literacy in Primary Education. (2023). *Reflecting Realities: Survey of Ethnic Representation Within UK Children's Literature 2023*. CLPE.

Cooperative Children's Book Center. (2023). *Books by and/or About Black, Indigenous and People of Color 2022*. School of Education, University of Wisconsin-Madison.

Cormier, C. J. (2024). Misidentification, misinformation, and miseducation: The experiences of minoritized students and representation in public schools across three societies around the globe. *Peabody Journal of Education, 99*(1), 1–3. https://doi.org/10.1080/0161956X.2024.2307792

Crisp, T., Knezek, S. M., Quinn, M., Bingham, G. E., Girardeau, K., & Starks, F. (2016). What's on our bookshelves? The diversity of children's literature in early childhood classroom libraries. *Journal of Children's Literature, 42*(2), 29–42.

Duke, N. K., & Cartwright, K. B. (2021). The science of reading progresses: Communicating advances beyond the simple view of reading. *Reading Research Quarterly, 56*(S1), S25–S44. https://doi.org/10.1002/rrq.411

Enriquez Watt, M., & Adam, H. (2023). *Research Impact Evidence Scheme: Research Impact: Dr Helen Adam*. Edith Cowan University.

Evans, S. (2010). The role of multicultural literature interactive read-alouds on student perspectives toward diversity. *Journal of Research in Innovative Teaching, 3*(1), 88–100.

First Book Research & Insights. (2023). *The Impact of a Diverse Classroom Library*. First Book.

Freebody, P., & Luke, A. (1990). Literacies programs: Debates and demands in cultural context. *Prospect: Australian Journal of TESOL, 5*(3), 7–16.

Friedman, J. (2022). Rapidly accelerating book bans are part of a coordinated assault on public education. *The Progressive, 86*(6), 31.

Harper, L. J., & Brand, S. T. (2010). More alike than different: Promoting respect through multicultural books and literacy strategies. *Childhood Education, 86*(4), 224–233. https://doi.org/10.1080/00094056.2010.10523153

Husband, T. (2012). Why can't Jamal read? *Phi Delta Kappan, 93*(5), 23–27. https://doi.org/10.1177/003172171209300506

Jackson-Barrett, E. (2021). Aboriginal children's literature: A time for healing? In H. Adam (Ed.), *Transforming Practice: Transforming Lives Through Diverse Children's Literature* (pp. 78–90). Primary English Teaching Association of Australia.

Karvelas, P. (2024, May 13). The Cumberland City Council book ban threatens to erase queer families. It's a threat that deserves a serious response. *ABC News*. https://www.abc.net.au/news/2024-05-13/cumberland-city-council-book-ban-threatens-erase-queer-families/103836256

Kidd, D. C., & Castano, E. (2013). Reading literary fiction improves theory of mind. *Science, 342*(6156), 377–380. https://doi.org/10.1126/science.1239918

Leggatt, A. (2022). What I needed when faced with a book ban. *The School Librarian, 70*(4), 14–15.

Luke, A., & Freebody, P. (1999). A map of possible practices: Further notes on the four resources model. *Practically Primary, 4*(2), 5–8.

Magos, K. (2018). "The neighbor's folktales": Developing intercultural competence through folktales and stories. *Bookbird, 56*(2), 28–34. https://doi.org/10.1353/bkb.2018.0023

Morrison, A., Rigney, L.-I., Hattam, R., & Diplock, A. (2019). *Toward an Australian Culturally Responsive Pedagogy: A Narrative Review of the Literature*. University of South Australia.

O'Keeffe, L., Paige, K., & Osborne, S. (2018). Getting started: Exploring pre-service teachers' confidence and knowledge of culturally responsive pedagogy in teaching mathematics and science. *Asia-Pacific Journal of Teacher Education, 47*(2), 152–175. https://doi.org/10.1080/1359866X.2018.1531386

PEN America. (2024). *Cover to Cover: An Analysis of Titles Banned in the 23–24 School Year*. PEN America.

Plastow, J., & Hillel, M. (2010). *The Sands of Time: Children's Literature: Culture, Politics & Identity*. University of Hertfordshire Press.

Sangrigoli, S., & De Schonen, S. (2004). Recognition of own-race and other-race faces by three-month-old infants. *Journal of Child Psychology and Psychiatry, 45*(7), 1219–1227. https://doi.org/10.1111/j.1469-7610.2004.00319.x

Short, K. (2012). Story as world making. *Language Arts, 90*(1), 9–17. https://doi.org/10.58680/la201220683

Souto-Manning, M., Boardman, A., Llerena, C., Martell, J., & Salas, A. (2018b). *No More Culturally Irrelevant Teaching*. Heinemann.

Souto-Manning, M., & Martell, J. (2016). *Reading, Writing, and Talk: Inclusive Teaching Strategies for Diverse Learners, K-2*. Teachers College Press.

Souto-Manning, M., Rabadi-Raol, A., Robinson, D., & Perez, A. (2018a). What stories do my classroom and its materials tell? Preparing early childhood teachers to engage in equitable and inclusive teaching. *Young Exceptional Children, 22*(2), 62–73. https://doi.org/10.1177/1096250618811619

Tatum, A. W. (2015). Engaging African American males in reading (Reprint). *Journal of Education*, *195*(2), 1–5. https://doi.org/10.1177/002205741519500202

Tatum, A. W., Johnson, A., & McMillon, D. (2021). The state of Black male literacy research, 1999–2020. *Literacy Research: Theory, Method, and Practice*, *70*(1), 129–151. https://doi.org/10.1177/23813377211038368

Tschida, C. M., Ryan, C. L., & Ticknor, A. S. (2014). Building on windows and mirrors: Encouraging the disruption of "single stories" through children's literature. *Journal of Children's Literature*, *40*(1), 28–39.

Zalusky, S. (2023). Beyond book bans. *Library Journal*, *148*(4), 14–16.

Disrupting Prejudice Through Children's Literature

6

Introduction

Having established in Chapter 5 that authentic representation in reading materials is essential for equitable literacy environments, this chapter examines how diverse literature can be actively employed as a tool for social transformation. The Model for Equitable Literacy Learning Environments (MELLE) positions literacy education not merely as skill acquisition but also as a vehicle for disrupting prejudice, challenging discrimination and cultivating inclusive attitudes from early childhood. While representation provides the necessary foundation by affirming children's identities and expanding their perspectives, critical literacy practices enable children to engage with literature in ways that actively confront bias and injustice. This chapter explores how diverse books, when approached through such critical practices, can counter the development of prejudice in ways that profoundly impact both individual children and broader society.

The Urgency of Early Intervention

Research establishes that children begin noticing racial differences from infancy, developing own-race bias as early as 3–6 months of age (Bar-Haim

DOI: 10.4324/9781003628217-6

et al., 2006; Sangrigoli & De Schonen, 2004). By ages 3–5, children start expressing social biases based on race and other visible differences. Critically, these early biases remain malleable and significantly influenced by environmental factors, including the books and stories children encounter (Aboud et al., 2012). Studies demonstrate that this bias can be disrupted through even brief exposure to diverse representations in pictures and literature (Bar-Haim et al., 2006).

The economic and social costs of prejudice are staggering. For example, racism costs the Australian economy approximately $37.9 billion AUD annually (Elias & Paradies, 2016), while prejudice against the LGBTQIA+ community incurs similar economic losses (Pride in Diversity, 2018). These costs primarily derive from the strong correlation between discrimination and negative health outcomes, particularly mental health challenges, including depression, anxiety, and post-traumatic stress disorder (Elias & Paradies, 2016, p. 4). Rather than waiting for these problems to emerge, by building inclusive communities in early childhood through literature, educators engage in transformative work that promotes social cohesion and mental wellbeing with far-reaching implications for society.

Critical Literacy as Anti-Bias Education

Drawing on Freire's (2000) critical pedagogy and Ladson-Billings's (2023) work on Critical Race Theory presented in Chapter 2, it is clear that literacy education exists within social, political and cultural contexts that can either perpetuate or challenge systems of oppression. Building on Chapter 5's discussion of Bishop's mirrors, windows and sliding glass doors metaphor, critical literacy practices extend the power of representation by guiding children to examine not just who is represented in texts, but how and why those representations exist. When positioned as a tool for analysing and confronting social inequities, critical literacy becomes essential for developing citizens who can interrogate and transform unjust social structures (Morrell, 2017). Derman-Sparks and Edwards's (2010) anti-bias education framework advocates for active intervention rather than passively hoping children naturally develop inclusive attitudes, with children's literature serving as a crucial tool by providing counternarratives to stereotypes and exposing children to diverse perspectives.

The most effective approaches to using children's literature for disrupting bias integrate Bishop's (1990) mirrors, windows and sliding glass doors metaphor with critical literacy practices. When children see themselves reflected in books (mirrors), they develop positive identity and belonging. When they encounter books about others (windows), they develop understanding and empathy. Through imaginative engagement (sliding glass doors), they emotionally connect with characters whose lives may initially seem far removed from their own. This integration directly supports children developing as text analysts in Freebody and Luke's Four Resources Model (1990) (discussed in Chapter 3), where children learn to critically examine the cultural assumptions and power relationships embedded in texts rather than accepting them as neutral reflections of reality. Paris and Alim's (2017) culturally sustaining pedagogy extends this framework by emphasising that education must actively sustain and foster cultural pluralism and equality. Within classrooms implementing these approaches, teachers facilitate critical discussions that help children examine how power, privilege and perspective operate in texts. Children learn to ask: Whose stories are being told? Whose voices are marginalised? How are different groups represented? What power relationships are portrayed?

Evidence confirms the effectiveness of this approach. Chapter 5 documented the academic and socioemotional benefits of diverse representation; these effects are amplified when children engage critically with diverse texts, developing not only stronger analytical skills but also deeper commitment to social justice. Further, Cameron et al. (2006) found that children reading stories featuring cross-group friendships showed significantly improved attitudes toward outgroup members, while Mar et al. (2009) demonstrated that exposure to narrative fiction correlates positively with empathic ability and social cognition. This critical literacy dimension is integral to all three components of the MELLE: quality instruction must support children's critical text analysis; opportunity ensures all children access transformative texts; and representation provides authentic content, enabling children to examine power structures.

The Imperative of the MELLE Beyond Literacy Skills

The convergence of research on early bias development, the substantial economic and health costs of prejudice, and evidence of literature's capacity to disrupt discrimination creates a compelling imperative for the MELLE. As established in Chapter 5, representation ensures children see themselves and diverse others authentically portrayed in reading materials. When this representation is paired with critical literacy approaches, children move from passive consumers of diverse content to active analysts and change agents. In this model, disrupting prejudice is positioned not as an additional educational goal but as intrinsic to equitable literacy education. Thus, when children develop reading skills alongside critical literacy capabilities, they become equipped not only to decode and comprehend texts but to analyse and challenge inequitable social structures. In the quality instruction dimension of MELLE, teachers are supported to possess the knowledge and pedagogical skills to facilitate critical discussions about power, privilege and perspective in literature. Through the opportunity dimension, all children, regardless of socioeconomic background, are provided access to texts that challenge their assumptions and expand their worldviews. Within the representation dimension, authentic, diverse content is provided that enables children to question stereotypes and examine how social structures shape lived experiences.

Evidence from classrooms implementing culturally responsive pedagogy demonstrates these approaches enhance rather than detract from academic achievement (Boutte et al., 2011; Husband, 2019; Paris & Alim, 2017). Children who engage critically with diverse literature develop stronger analytical skills, deeper comprehension abilities and more nuanced understanding of narrative structures (Cameron et al., 2006; Mar et al., 2009). Simultaneously, they develop empathy, cultural competence and commitment to social justice—qualities essential for creating more equitable societies (Derman-Sparks & Edwards, 2010; Morrell, 2017). However, research confirms that teachers often feel underprepared to address issues of race and discrimination with young children—reinforcing the need for integrated professional development that addresses both technical and critical dimensions of literacy instruction (Adam, 2021; Husband, 2019).

Conclusion: Literature as Lever for Social Transformation

The evidence presented in this chapter demonstrates that children's literature, approached through critical literacy practices, represents a powerful tool for disrupting prejudice and challenging discrimination before these attitudes become entrenched. By addressing bias in education settings through literature, educators engage in work that transcends traditional educational boundaries to disrupt racism and impact public health, economic outcomes and social cohesion. In the MELLE, this transformative potential is recognised as central rather than peripheral to equitable literacy education. When quality instruction, opportunity to read and representation work together within contexts of critical literacy, children develop not merely as readers but also as informed, empathetic citizens capable of challenging and transforming inequitable social structures. This chapter connects the theoretical foundations established in Chapter 2 with the practical applications that follow in Chapter 7, illustrating how the model's dimensions converge to create learning environments where literacy serves both academic excellence and social justice.

The following chapter will present the MELLE in comprehensive detail, integrating these insights into a practical guide for implementation across diverse educational contexts.

References

Aboud, F. E., Tredoux, C., Tropp, L. R., Brown, C. S., Niens, U., & Noor, N. M. (2012). Interventions to reduce prejudice and enhance inclusion and respect for ethnic differences in early childhood: A systematic review. *Developmental Review*, *32*(4), 307–336. https://doi.org/10.1016/j.dr.2012.05.001

Adam, H. (2021). When authenticity goes missing: How monocultural children's literature is silencing the voices and contributing to invisibility of children from minority backgrounds. *Education Sciences*, *11*(1), 32. https://doi.org/10.3390/educsci11010032

Bar-Haim, Y., Ziv, T., Lamy, D., & Hodes, R. M. (2006). Nature and nurture in own-race face processing. *Psychological Science*, *17*(2), 159–163. https://doi.org/10.1111/j.1467-9280.2006.01679.x

Bishop, R. S. (1990). Mirrors, windows, and sliding glass doors. *Perspectives*, *6*(3), ix–xi.

Boutte, G. S., Lopez-Robertson, J., & Powers-Costello, E. (2011). Moving beyond colorblindness in early childhood classrooms. *Early Childhood Education Journal*, *39*(5), 335–342. https://doi.org/10.1007/s10643-011-0457-x

Cameron, L., Rutland, A., Brown, R., & Douch, R. (2006). Changing children's intergroup attitudes toward refugees: Testing different models of extended contact. *Child Development*, *77*(5), 1208–1219. https://doi.org/10.1111/j.1467-8624.2006.00929.x

Derman-Sparks, L., & Edwards, J. O. (2010). *Anti-bias Education for Young Children and Ourselves*. National Association for the Education of Young Children.

Elias, A., & Paradies, Y. (2016). The costs of institutional racism and its ethical implications for healthcare. *Journal of Bioethical Inquiry*, *13*(4), 577–590. https://doi.org/10.1007/s11673-020-10073-0

Freebody, P., & Luke, A. (1990). Literacies programs: Debates and demands in cultural context. *Prospect: Australian Journal of TESOL*, *5*(3), 7–16.

Freire, P. (2000). *Pedagogy of the Oppressed* (30th anniversary ed.). Continuum.

Husband, T. (2019). Using multicultural picture books to promote racial justice in urban early childhood literacy classrooms. *Urban Education, 54*(8), 1058–1084. https://doi.org/10.1177/0042085918805145

Ladson-Billings, G. (2023). Just what is critical race theory and what's it doing in a nice field like education? In E. Taylor, D. Gillborn, & G. Ladson-Billings (Eds.), *Foundations of Critical Race Theory in Education* (3rd ed.). Routledge. https://doi.org/10.4324/b23210

Mar, R. A., Oatley, K., & Peterson, J. B. (2009). Exploring the link between reading fiction and empathy: Ruling out individual differences and examining outcomes. *Communications, 34*(4), 407–428. https://doi.org/10.1515/COMM.2009.025

Morrell, E. (2017). Toward equity and diversity in literacy research, policy, and practice: A critical, global approach. *Journal of Literacy Research, 49*(3), 454–463. https://doi.org/10.1177/1086296X17720963

Paris, D., & Alim, H. S. (Eds.). (2017). *Culturally Sustaining Pedagogies: Teaching and Learning for Justice in a Changing World*. Teachers College Press. https://doi.org/10.22329/jtl.v11i1.4987

Pride in Diversity. (2018). *Australian Workplace Equality Index*. ACON.

Sangrigoli, S., & De Schonen, S. (2004). Recognition of own-race and other-race faces by three-month-old infants. *Journal of Child Psychology and Psychiatry, 45*(7), 1219–1227. https://doi.org/10.1111/j.1469-7610.2004.00319.x

The Model for Equitable Literacy Learning Environments

7

Introduction: Bringing the Dimensions Together

The preceding chapters have explored the theoretical foundations for equitable literacy education (Chapters 1 and 2), examined the challenges of quality instruction (Chapter 3), analysed opportunity disparities (Chapter 4), discussed the critical importance of representation in reading materials (Chapter 5) and explored how literature can disrupt prejudice (Chapter 6). This chapter brings these threads together to present the Model for Equitable Literacy Learning Environments (MELLE) (Figure 7.1), first introduced in Chapter 2, as a comprehensive framework that integrates these dimensions into a cohesive approach for practice.

The core of the MELLE consists of three interlocking dimensions: Quality Instruction, Opportunity and Representation. While each dimension contains several important aspects to be addressed in practice, the interlocking nature of these three dimensions highlights that for truly equitable education these dimensions cannot function effectively in isolation. Quality instruction without considering aspects of representation risks alienating children from diverse backgrounds. Ample reading opportunities without quality instruction overlooks the importance of explicit teaching of literacy skills. Diverse representation without opportunities for engagement with texts limits its impact. As illustrated in Figure 7.1, these three core dimensions operate within broader contextual factors of culture, community, context and curriculum—highlighting that equitable literacy instruction is not simply a matter of implementing specific classroom techniques

DOI: 10.4324/9781003628217-7

The Model for Equitable Literacy Learning Environments 93

Figure 7.1 The model for equitable literacy learning environments.

94 Creating Equitable Literacy Learning Environments

but also involves responsive practice within specific social and institutional contexts. This chapter explores the integrated nature of the MELLE, focusing particularly on how the dimensions interconnect and reinforce each other within these broader environments. Practical applications are then provided for educators, demonstrating how the model can be implemented across diverse classrooms. Through vignettes of successful implementation and guidance on measuring outcomes beyond standardised test scores, this chapter offers a roadmap for transformative literacy education environments that serve all children.

Dimension Intersections: The Power of Integration

The power of the MELLE lies in the intersections of its three core dimensions. These intersections create synergistic effects that enhance literacy learning beyond what any single dimension can accomplish alone.

Quality Instruction and Opportunity Intersection

When quality instruction intersects with opportunity, children's skill development is supported by meaningful application and practice. Evidence-based teaching approaches become more effective when children have ample opportunities to apply their developing skills through engagement with diverse, engaging texts. This intersection creates several important benefits:

- Explicit phonics instruction is reinforced when children have time to practice decoding in both decodable and self-selected books that interest them
- Comprehension strategies taught through explicit instruction become meaningful when children apply them to texts they choose during independent reading time
- Vocabulary instruction has greater impact when children encounter and use new words in varied reading contexts
- Fluency development requires substantial reading practice with appropriately challenging texts, which can only occur when sufficient time and materials are provided

This intersection addresses a common disconnect in literacy education where children may be taught reading skills but given insufficient opportunities to apply them in authentic contexts. As established in Chapter 4, children who have more opportunities to read develop greater fluency and comprehension than those who spend most of their instructional time on isolated skill practice (Allington, 2014). More recent research reinforces these findings, confirming that independent reading opportunities enhance both reading attitudes and achievement, particularly benefiting developing readers (Bus et al., 2024; Cremin & Scholes, 2024).

For children who may have limited access to books outside school, this intersection is particularly critical for developing reading proficiency. As demonstrated in Chapter 4, structured independent reading opportunities with appropriate guidance and support are especially beneficial for children at risk of reading failure (Merke et al., 2024). When quality instruction provides the skills and strategies children need, and opportunity provides the time and resources to apply these skills, children develop both technical proficiency and reading motivation. The work of Cremin et al. (2014), discussed in Chapter 4, further illustrates how teachers who develop rich knowledge of children's literature and create engaging reading environments help children build positive reader identities alongside technical skills. This intersection thus supports not just short-term skill acquisition, but long-term development as engaged, confident readers.

Quality Instruction and Representation Intersection

When quality instruction intersects with representation, children's engagement with evidence-based practices is enhanced through culturally responsive practice. Building on the evidence presented in Chapters 3 and 5, this intersection creates several significant educational benefits:

- It makes abstract skills concrete through culturally relevant contexts
- It validates children's identities and experiences as worthy of academic attention
- It harnesses children's linguistic repertoires
- It provides and builds on background knowledge that supports comprehension
- It increases engagement by connecting literacy learning to children's lives
- It builds bridges between school literacy practices and home literacy experiences

This intersection transforms how foundational skills are taught by embedding them in meaningful cultural contexts. For example, as explored in Chapter 3, phonics instruction becomes more effective when it acknowledges linguistic diversity and builds connections to children's home languages and dialects. Wright et al. (2022) emphasise that quality phonemic awareness and phonics instruction must acknowledge linguistic diversity rather than imposing a single standard, noting that "teachers who are committed to fostering belonging talk about variation as an inherent part of language" (p. 69).

Similarly, comprehension instruction benefits from culturally diverse texts that allow children to activate their existing knowledge while learning new strategies. As established in Chapter 5, when literacy instruction incorporates children's cultural and linguistic resources, children show greater engagement, stronger comprehension and more positive literacy identities. For children from marginalised backgrounds, seeing their languages and cultural practices valued in instruction can transform their relationship to literacy learning. A positive example of this is evident in Duke et al.'s (2021) Layered Model of Comprehension Instruction (see Figure 7.2) which provides a supportive model that aligns with the MELLE positioning cultural knowledge as a key component of comprehension development, recognising that children's cultural backgrounds provide valuable resources for making meaning from texts.

The First Book Research & Insights study (2023), discussed in Chapter 5, provides compelling evidence for this intersection, showing that classrooms using culturally diverse books within their literacy instruction demonstrated significant improvements in reading assessment scores, with the lowest-performing students showing the greatest gains. This suggests that representation is not merely a matter of inclusion but also a powerful pedagogical tool that enhances the effectiveness of evidence-based instruction. When quality instruction is delivered through texts and contexts that authentically represent diverse experiences, children develop not only technical skills but also positive relationships with reading and strong literacy identities. This intersection thus addresses both the cognitive and affective dimensions of literacy development, creating more equitable and effective learning environments for all children.

Opportunity and Representation Intersection

When opportunity intersects with representation, children have access not just to books but to books that reflect diverse identities and experiences. Building on the evidence presented in Chapters 4 and 5, this intersection creates several powerful educational benefits:

The Model for Equitable Literacy Learning Environments 97

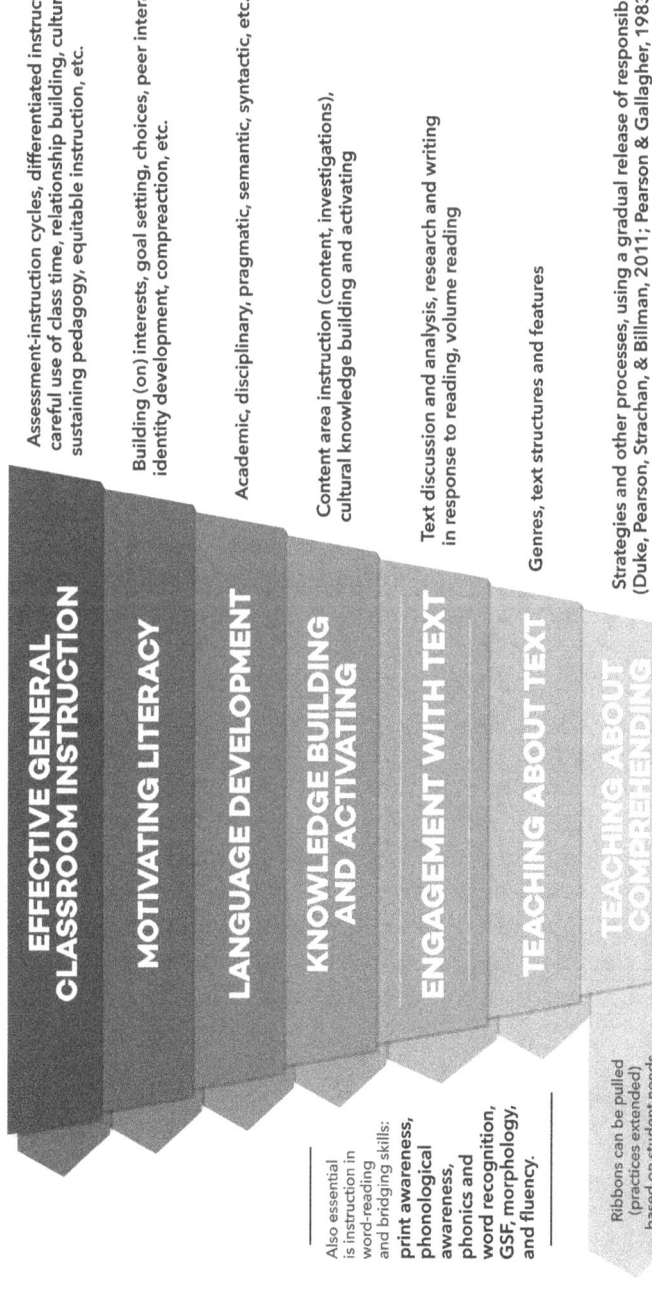

Figure 7.2 The Layered Model of Comprehension Instruction (Duke, Ward and Pearson, 2021).
Reprinted from Duke, N. K., Ward, A. E., & Pearson, P. D. The Science of Reading Comprehension Instruction. *The Reading Teacher*, 74(6), 663–672. Copyright 2021 Authors. Reprinted with permission.

- It increases motivation by providing texts in which children see themselves
- It expands horizons by introducing children to diverse perspectives
- It builds empathy through windows into others' experiences
- It challenges stereotypes through authentic portrayals of diverse groups
- It creates entry points for children who might otherwise disengage from reading

For children from marginalised backgrounds, this intersection addresses the double disadvantage many face: limited access to books in general, and even more limited access to books that reflect their experiences. As demonstrated in Chapter 5, when children from underrepresented groups encounter books that authentically reflect their identities, they show greater engagement and more positive attitudes towards reading. The First Book Research & Insights study (2023) also demonstrated that alongside improvements in reading assessment scores, children increased their reading time by an additional 4 hours per week on average when provided with diverse, representative texts. This significant increase in reading volume directly addresses the opportunity gap identified in Chapter 4. Further, Cremin and Scholes' (2024) critical review of the reading for pleasure evidence base, discussed in Chapter 4, highlights that access to diverse, engaging texts is a matter of social justice. They note that "being a reader in childhood can play a role in reducing educational inequalities" (p. 538), particularly when children have access to books that reflect their own experiences while also introducing them to others' perspectives.

This intersection is a reminder that it is not sufficient to simply provide books; the nature of representation in books provided must be considered, as must be whether or not they offer both mirrors in which children can see themselves and windows through which they can view diverse experiences. When children have opportunities to engage with texts that authentically represent diverse identities and perspectives, they are more likely to develop both the skills and the motivation to become lifelong readers.

The Central Intersection—the Child: Where All Dimensions Meet

The most powerful learning occurs at the central intersection where all three dimensions converge. In this space, children receive quality instruction through culturally responsive approaches, have ample opportunities to engage with books, and see themselves and others authentically represented in those books. This comprehensive approach supports both technical reading skills and the development of positive reader identities. For example, a teacher who explicitly teaches comprehension strategies using diverse texts, provides time for independent reading of a wide range of books, and ensures the classroom library includes authentic representation of various cultures and experiences is working at this central intersection. In such environments, all children can develop as readers who are both technically proficient and also personally engaged with reading.

Contextual Dimensions: The Environment for Implementation

The three core dimensions of the MELLE operate within broader contexts that shape their implementation and impact. Rather than viewing these contextual factors as background elements, the MELLE positions them as active part of the framework that significantly influence how the core dimensions are understood and enacted in specific settings.

Culture/s

Cultural contexts—both the institutional cultures of schools and the cultures of the communities they serve—shape how literacy is defined, taught and assessed. A school's cultural values regarding diversity significantly influence MELLE implementation, with inclusive schools finding this more straightforward than those oriented towards uniformity. Within the MELLE, cultural context informs quality instruction approaches, valued reading opportunities, and authentic representation. In communities with strong oral storytelling traditions, instruction should harness these narratives as bridges to print literacy, using them to develop comprehension and as foundations for student and community-made books. Jackson-Barrett and Lee-Hammond (2019) show how Country itself can serve as text and pedagogical resource, enabling children to connect cultural knowledge with literacy development. In multilingual communities, literacy opportunities should include multi-language texts, emphasising linguistic diversity and validating children's full linguistic repertoires.

Community

The MELLE encompasses recognition that equitable literacy education requires partnerships with families and communities and the importance of literacy practices extending beyond school settings. Community perspectives inform quality instruction by providing insights into children's home literacy experiences, extend reading opportunities beyond the classroom, and ensure authentic representation through community input on resources and curricula. Effective implementation of the MELLE involves approaches such as family literacy programmes, community book drives, partnerships with local libraries and the inclusion of community members as cultural consultants and classroom resources. These approaches position families not as recipients of school-determined literacy practices but as valuable knowledge-holders and partners in children's literacy development.

Context

Educational contexts—including school demographics, location, available resources and institutional priorities—significantly influence how the MELLE dimensions can be implemented. Each setting presents unique considerations that shape practice:

- Urban, suburban, or rural settings with varying resource access
- Student demographics, including cultural, linguistic, and socioeconomic diversity
- School missions and priorities
- Physical environments and available spaces
- Historical relationships between schools and communities

Recent evidence from the University of New South Wales demonstrates how central context is to accurate assessment. Dobrescu et al. (2022) found that simply adapting National Assessment Program – Literacy and Numeracy (NAPLAN) questions to include contextually familiar references for Aboriginal and rural students could close the Indigenous reading gap by up to 50% and reduce urban–rural disparities by a third. This powerful evidence, which will be discussed further in Chapter 9, illustrates that what we often measure as 'achievement gaps' may actually be artifacts of culturally biased assessment rather than true differences in knowledge or ability.

A highly diverse urban school with students from "over forty" cultural backgrounds (as mentioned in one of the vignettes to follow) may require different implementation strategies than a more homogeneous setting. For example, a school with many English language learners might emphasise multilingual texts and approaches, while a school with limited book access might prioritise building robust classroom libraries, while a school with limited diversity may prioritise expanding the worldviews of their students.

Curriculum

The MELLE encompasses the understanding that literacy instruction occurs within curriculum frameworks that may either support or constrain equitable approaches. National, state and local curriculum requirements influence what is taught, how it is assessed, and which resources are used. Educators implementing the model can work to align curriculum requirements with equitable practices, advocating for flexibility where necessary to meet diverse learners' needs.

Recent developments in Australian curriculum frameworks show promising movement towards greater emphasis on critical literacy, exemplified by ACARA's (2025) *Media consumers and creators resource*. This initiative represents growing recognition of the importance of developing students' capacity as text analysts—a key component of the Quality Instruction dimension of the MELLE. As discussed in Chapter 3, the text analyst role enables students to critically examine how texts position readers and reflect power structures in society. By integrating these critical literacy practices into curriculum frameworks, educational systems create more opportunities for students to recognise bias, question dominant narratives and challenge inequitable representations.

The curriculum context also affects scheduling and delivery of quality instruction, integration of reading opportunities into the school day, and selection of texts that provide authentic representation. Effective implementation requires identifying spaces within existing curriculum frameworks where equitable practices can flourish. Together, these contextual dimensions create the environment in which the three core dimensions operate. Successful implementation of the MELLE requires attention to these broader contexts and their influence on quality instruction, opportunity, and representation.

Vignettes of Integration

The following vignettes illustrate how the MELLE's dimensions can be integrated in practice across diverse educational settings. Each example demonstrates multiple dimensions of the framework operating simultaneously within specific contextual environments.

Vignette 1: Culturally Responsive Literature in a Diverse Primary School

In a primary school in a highly diverse suburb of the Perth metropolitan area, Western Australia, teacher Keyan works with students from over forty different cultural backgrounds. His approach illustrates the integration of all three MELLE dimensions within a highly diverse context. Keyan carefully selects texts that reflect his students' diverse backgrounds and creates opportunities for meaningful engagement with these materials:

> When it comes to exposure to literature that represents students, I am constantly trying to locate literature that highlights differences in culture as well as home life and what we define as 'family'. Clearly, in this school, there is no true definition of 'normal'.

When introducing *The Proudest Blue* (Muhammad & Ali, 2019), a book about a young Muslim girl's first day wearing a hijab, Keyan observed:

> One student's mother and sister wear a hijab, and he shared a huge amount of enthusiasm and joy when he saw characters that he could relate to. He struggles in literacy, and it was fantastic to see him so engaged and proud of his family/culture when we began reading.

This example demonstrates all three dimensions of the MELLE working together:

- **Quality Instruction**: Keyan embeds reading skills development within culturally relevant content, making learning meaningful and accessible
- **Opportunity**: He provides access to diverse books and time for engagement with texts that connect to students' lives
- **Representation**: He selects texts that authentically reflect his students' diverse backgrounds and experiences

The contextual dimensions are also evident. The school's cultural context includes extraordinary diversity, requiring particularly thoughtful attention to representation. The community context involves families from many different cultural backgrounds, whose cultural practices (like wearing a hijab) become validated through classroom literacy practices. The curricular context allows for thematic connections between books:

> We really tied this to *My Shadow is Pink/Purple*. (Stuart, 2020, 2022) (These are books that gently challenge gender diversity and stereotypes). We discussed how the bullies in that story didn't have any 'colour' and were blacked out in 'black/white noise'. One student speculated 'Maybe they don't know the colour of their shadow/themselves?'

This integration of dimensions and contexts creates a learning environment where all students, regardless of background, can engage meaningfully with literacy while developing technical skills, positive reader identities and critical literacy dispositions.

Vignette 2: The Transformative Power of Representation

A powerful example of dimension integration comes from Preservice Teacher, Maya's observation of a young Sikh boy in a Year 3 classroom.

> He wore a Patka (a child's turban), was quite petite, and spoke softly. Despite being academically capable, he hesitated to participate in class discussions. The teacher (herself a member of the Indian diaspora) noticed that he seemed very aware of his physical appearance and difference, and she suspected he had been teased by peers, which made him even more withdrawn.
>
> To address this, she chose to read a book titled *I Am Sikh* (Nixon & Fairclough, 2008) as part of a literacy unit. The book shares a young Sikh boy's story, exploring his identity, the significance of his Patka, and the contributions of Sikhs to community, sports, agriculture and beyond—both in India and globally.

The results were transformative:

> The boy began to open up. His peers began to understand and respect his culture, and slowly, he started participating more actively in class. His academic and social confidence grew visibly and rapidly.

The teacher's response integrated all three MELLE dimensions, illustrating

- **Quality Instruction**: The teacher embedded literacy learning within culturally responsive content, teaching reading skills while addressing social dynamics

- **Opportunity**: She provided access to a book that specifically reflected an underrepresented student's identity and experience
- **Representation**: She selected a text that authentically portrayed Sikh identity and culture, validating the student's background

The contextual dimensions are equally evident. The cultural context included potential prejudice that was addressed through literacy education. The classroom community was transformed through greater understanding and respect. The teacher adapted the curriculum context to include culturally relevant content that served both academic and social purposes. This case powerfully demonstrates how attention to representation can transform the educational experience of a marginalised student while simultaneously enriching learning for all students in the class.

Vignette 3: Student Agency and Cultural Leadership

This third vignette illustrates how student agency can enhance the implementation of the MELLE. When Kate, a preservice teacher working in a school with a diverse population including many Aboriginal students, gave her students choice in selecting read-aloud books, she discovered the power of positioning students as cultural leaders:

> The girls were so enthusiastic and asked if they could choose more books for me to read aloud. They chose a book by Adam Goodes and another by Cathy Freeman[1]…they seemed to want to know more about their Aboriginal heroes.

This led to a transformative classroom dynamic:

> They asked me how much I knew about their culture, and I said not as much as them and that they too could share their stories with us. The Aboriginal girls proceeded to share their stories and knowledge of their culture. It was incredible. The children themselves are aware of what is authentic; they knew how to predict with enthusiasm but more so, they did not fault me as a person from a non-Aboriginal background to admit that I am not as well equipped in the full knowledge of their rich histories and cultures, and that I am still learning.

By acknowledging the limits of her own cultural knowledge and positioning the Aboriginal students as experts, Kate created an opportunity for these students to take on leadership roles:

> The children themselves are aware of what is authentic…This gave them the opportunity to share more…and those kids had fire when I admitted that they have a lot to teach us too.

This example demonstrates how teachers can position themselves as co-learners, acknowledging the limits of their knowledge while creating spaces for students to share their cultural expertise.

This example demonstrates:

- **Quality Instruction**: Kate supported literacy development through authentic dialogue about culturally relevant texts
- **Opportunity**: She provided access to books that reflected Aboriginal identities and experiences, allowing student choice in selection
- **Representation**: The books featured Aboriginal role models, and student voices further enriched representation through personal storytelling
- **Reflective Practice**: Kate reflected on her own practice and considered how to draw on the children's strengths and funds of knowledge

The contextual dimensions were similarly addressed. The cultural context allowed for recognition of Aboriginal perspectives and knowledge. The community context expanded as students shared their cultural knowledge. The teacher adapted the educational context to position students as knowledge-holders rather than mere recipients of information.

This case illustrates how the MELLE can be implemented in ways that not only support literacy development but also empower students from often-marginalised backgrounds to share their cultural knowledge and take on leadership roles.

Vignette 4: Integrating Quality Instruction with Engaging and Diverse Texts

From teacher Mitchell comes an example of how quality instruction and opportunity can be thoughtfully integrated. Mitchell explains his approach to literacy instruction in his Year 2 classroom:

> When I think how I am going to provide opportunities for kids to engage with books, I do so with the goal of fostering a genuine joy for reading. I have incorporated a decodable book series into my Year 2 reading groups. The series consists of ten books, each focusing on different phonics sounds while contributing to a larger, continuous story.

> Each day, I work with the groups on phonological awareness, vocabulary, comprehension, and reading fluency. What's been especially encouraging is the students' excitement to pick up where the story left off each week. The series features a diverse cast of characters, varying in age, gender, and ethnicity, who navigate an ongoing plot that often ends with a cliffhanger. It's been wonderful to see the students genuinely enjoying the narrative and becoming eager to discover how the story develops.

Mitchell's approach demonstrates the integration of systematic phonics instruction with engagement and representation. By selecting decodable texts that feature diverse characters and compelling narratives, he ensures students develop essential skills while building reading motivation.

His comprehensive literacy approach extends beyond decodable texts:

> What has been further encouraging is the incorporation of Shared Reading in the mornings. During the first two days of the week, we simply read for the pleasure of it. These sessions spark rich conversations about the story, and we often extend our understanding through roleplay activities such as character hot seats. In this game, students take on the role of a character from the book, and the class interviews them, encouraging deeper thinking and empathy for the characters. This has proven to be a highly engaging way to develop oral language, comprehension, and confidence. Following this, we delve into the vocabulary, phonics and fluency for the following three days respectively. It's important to note that when choosing a 'big book' for Shared Reading, I strive to ensure that there is a rich and engaging narrative (with a hint of predictability and patterns throughout) with authentic, diverse representations.

Mitchell has also created a classroom environment that provides ample opportunity for independent reading:

> When setting up my classroom, I've always made it a priority to include a reading corner filled with a wide variety of accessible, high-quality texts. My collection has grown over time to feature books that reflect diverse characters, cultures, and stories. I hope that such a collection will enable students see themselves and others in what they read. I often found that at first the children were drawn to the funny and silly books, which served as a great hook! But over time, they've started seeking out stories by their favourite authors, series they enjoy and scenarios they can relate to.

Mitchell further addresses accessibility through technology:

> Accessibility has also been a key focus. In addition to physical books, the corner includes iPads allowing students to scan QR codes to access eBooks and have stories read aloud to them. This has been especially helpful for students who aren't yet confident with independent reading but still love engaging with stories. I have found that the eBook titles alone, like *Zombies Don't Eat Veggies* and *Hey, That's My Monster!*, often spark their curiosity and excitement to read.

This vignette illustrates all three dimensions of the MELLE framework:

- **Quality Instruction**: Mitchell implements systematic phonics instruction supported by decodable texts while also teaching vocabulary, comprehension and fluency
- **Opportunity**: He provides multiple opportunities for engagement with texts, including guided reading groups, shared reading and independent reading in a well-resourced reading corner
- **Representation**: He intentionally selects texts featuring diverse characters and perspectives, ensuring all students see themselves and others in what they read

Mitchell's approach demonstrates that evidence-based reading instruction and reading engagement need not be opposing forces. By thoughtfully integrating systematic skill development with authentic reading experiences and diverse representation, he creates a literacy environment that supports both technical proficiency and reading motivation.

Vignette 5: Systemic Approaches: Teacher Education and Policy Frameworks

The implementation of the MELLE framework requires not only changes in classroom practice but also transformation of how teachers are prepared and how educational policies are formulated. The following examples illustrate how systemic approaches can create enabling conditions for equitable literacy education.

The University of South Carolina's Urban Education Cohort,[2] led by Professor Gloria Boutte, provides a powerful example of how Initial Teacher Education (ITE) can be redesigned to centre culturally responsive pedagogy. This pioneering programme within the Bachelor of Arts in Early Childhood Education explicitly focuses on developing teacher leaders with expertise in early childhood curriculum, instruction, and assessment through an in-depth focus on equity issues such as race, ethnicity, language diversity, sexual orientation, and gender identification and a particular emphasis on countering racial bias in and out of schools.

(University of South Carolina, 2023)

During my Churchill Fellowship, I observed graduates of this programme implementing all three dimensions of the MELLE framework in their classrooms. In one Grade Three classroom serving predominantly African American students, a recent graduate had taught her students the concepts of "mirrors and windows" as analytical tools for examining representation in literature. The children actively used this framework to identify when they saw themselves reflected in texts and when texts offered perspectives on others' experiences. More importantly, they had developed the critical consciousness to recognise and articulate when they or their peers were invisible in curriculum materials. This approach to preparation equips teachers with both the theoretical understanding and practical strategies to implement quality instruction informed by culturally responsive pedagogy. The programme places significant emphasis on the selection and use of diverse books and resources, addressing the representation dimension of the MELLE framework. By grounding instruction in students' lived experiences and cultural knowledge, these teachers create learning environments where all students can thrive.

At the policy level, Scotland provides an exemplary model of how professional standards and accreditation requirements can establish culturally responsive practice as a core expectation rather than an optional approach. The General Teaching Council for Scotland (GTCS) has embedded principles of equity and inclusion throughout their professional standards and Initial Teacher Education accreditation guidelines (2019). Unlike approaches that position cultural responsiveness as a separate competency area, the Scottish model foregrounds these principles as central to all domains of teacher practice. The Scottish Graduate Teacher Requirements explicitly requires that teachers commit "to social justice through fair, transparent, inclusive and sustainable policies and practices in relation to protected characteristics… and intersectionality" (The General Teaching Council for Scotland, 2021). This systemic approach ensures that culturally responsive pedagogy is not perceived as an add-on but as fundamental to quality teaching.

Education Scotland has further strengthened this approach through professional learning initiatives such as the Building Racial Literacy programme, which provides in-service teachers with structured support for developing culturally responsive practice. This multilayered approach—encompassing pre-service preparation, professional standards and continuing professional development—creates a coherent system that values and prioritises equity in education. The Scottish example illustrates how policy frameworks can create enabling conditions for implementing the MELLE framework at scale, demonstrating that systemic change requires alignment between classroom practice, teacher preparation and regulatory frameworks. By embedding cultural responsiveness within core professional standards rather than treating it as an optional specialisation, Scotland has created a model that recognises equity as central to educational quality.

These systemic approaches demonstrate that implementing the MELLE framework is not just about individual teacher practice but requires supportive structures at institutional and policy levels. When teacher education programmes prioritise culturally responsive pedagogy and policy frameworks embed equity principles, educators are better prepared and supported to create truly equitable literacy environments for all students.

Implementing the MELLE in Practice

Translating the MELLE from theoretical framework to classroom reality requires thoughtful attention to teaching practices, assessment approaches and practical strategies for addressing implementation challenges. Rather than treating these as separate domains, effective implementation integrates them into a cohesive approach that addresses all dimensions of the model simultaneously.

Teaching Practice as the Foundation for Implementation

The vignettes presented earlier demonstrate how teaching practice—the ways educators engage with children daily—forms the essential foundation for implementing the MELLE. Effective implementation begins with critical reflection on personal biases and assumptions about literacy, learning and diversity. As seen in Kate's acknowledgment of her limited knowledge of Aboriginal culture, this reflective stance creates space for more authentic interactions with students. When educators examine how their own cultural backgrounds shape their perceptions of children's literacy practices, they can question taken-for-granted assumptions about 'good' literacy instruction and remain open to diverse ways of knowing. Collaborative planning extends this reflective practice by incorporating multiple perspectives from colleagues, families and community members. Mitchell's approach to literacy instruction illustrates how this collaboration influenced his selection of diverse texts and instructional strategies. By ensuring that diverse viewpoints inform instructional decisions, educators create more inclusive learning environments that respond to the needs and strengths of all students.

Ongoing professional learning focused on culturally responsive literacy practices sustains implementation efforts over time. The University of South Carolina's Urban Education Cohort exemplifies how structured initial teacher education can equip pre-service teachers with both theoretical understanding and practical strategies for implementing all dimensions of the MELLE. This Bachelor of Arts in Early Childhood Education programme explicitly focuses on developing teacher leaders with expertise in equity issues and countering racial bias.

Beyond initial preparation, in-service teachers require continuing professional development that is collaborative and directly connected to classroom practice. This ongoing learning helps practising educators develop the knowledge, skills and dispositions needed for culturally responsive literacy instruction. Finally, advocacy for supportive policies and resources becomes an essential part of implementation. Keyan's persistent efforts to locate literature that highlights cultural differences illustrates how individual teachers often must advocate for the resources needed to create truly inclusive literacy environments. Collective advocacy at school, district and policy levels can amplify these efforts, creating system-wide support for equitable literacy education.

Holistic Assessment for Equitable Literacy Development

Traditional assessment approaches that focus solely on discrete skills often miss critical aspects of literacy development, particularly for children from diverse backgrounds. Implementing the MELLE requires assessment approaches that capture the multidimensional nature of literacy and align with the model's values. Comprehensive assessment within this framework should balance academic measures of reading proficiency with indicators of engagement, critical literacy and equity. While standardised assessments provide valuable benchmark data, their interpretation must consider the cultural contexts in which literacy develops. As the research from the University of New South Wales, discussed earlier, demonstrated, contextualised assessment can dramatically reduce measured 'achievement gaps,' suggesting that what appear to be literacy deficits may actually reflect culturally biased assessment instruments.

Further, by tracking indicators such as motivation, volume of reading and expressions of reading identity, educators can gain insight into aspects of literacy development that profoundly influence long-term outcomes. For example, the Reading Engagement Scale (McGeown & Conrad Smith, 2024) demonstrates how engagement—an important dimension often overlooked in traditional assessment—can be reliably measured. In Mitchell's classroom, students' excitement to continue reading series books, and their growing preferences for particular authors and genres, provide tangible evidence of developing reading engagement.

Rather than treating critical literacy and cultural responsiveness as separate domains for assessment, educators can embed observation of these dimensions within everyday literacy activities. The Year 3 classroom where students applied the 'mirrors and windows' framework to analyse representation in texts demonstrates how critical literacy can be assessed authentically through classroom discussions and activities. Throughout all assessment approaches, the goal remains educational equity—ensuring that all children have opportunities to develop as readers regardless of background. By monitoring patterns of access, participation and achievement across different demographic groups, educators can identify and address systemic barriers to equitable literacy development. This monitoring extends beyond analysing test scores to examining how the entire literacy environment serves diverse learners.

Strategic Resource Allocation and Development

The resource constraints faced by many schools create difficult choices in implementing comprehensive approaches or models like the MELLE, yet the vignettes demonstrate how educators can make strategic decisions that advance equity even within limited resource environments. By conducting regular audits of existing collections using frameworks such as those presented in Chapter 5, educators can identify representation gaps and make strategic acquisitions that address the most pressing needs—as exemplified by Mitchell's gradual development of a classroom library featuring "books that reflect diverse characters, cultures, and stories." This approach to resource development acknowledges that diverse book collections form a crucial foundation for implementation, providing both mirrors and windows for all students while recognising that acquisition must be strategic rather than haphazard. Time allocation represents another critical resource consideration, as quality instruction requires dedicated periods for explicit teaching while the opportunity dimension necessitates protected time for independent reading and engagement with diverse texts. Mitchell's classroom schedule demonstrates how thoughtful organisation can address both dimensions simultaneously rather than treating them as competing priorities, creating space for both shared reading and independent exploration within the constraints of the school day.

Professional learning and community partnerships further extend implementation capacity when financial resources are limited. When traditional professional development opportunities are constrained, teacher-led learning communities can leverage existing expertise within schools, creating sustainable structures for knowledge sharing and ongoing professional growth through mentoring relationships between more and less experienced practitioners. These communities of practice allow for incremental capacity building without requiring significant financial investment. Similarly, strategic partnerships with libraries, cultural organisations and community members provide valuable access to cultural knowledge and additional book resources that schools might otherwise be unable to afford. Kate's approach of inviting Aboriginal students to share their cultural knowledge exemplifies how community expertise can enrich literacy instruction when educators position themselves as co-learners rather than sole knowledge-holders—a stance that not only addresses resource constraints but also transforms power relationships within the classroom. This broader conceptualisation of resources—encompassing financial assets, time allocation, professional expertise and community knowledge—provides a framework through which educational institutions might implement the MELLE's core dimensions despite significant material constraints.

Navigating Implementation Challenges

While the MELLE presents quality instruction, opportunity and representation as interlocking dimensions that mutually reinforce one another, real-world implementation often reveals tensions between these elements. Implementing the MELLE inevitably involves navigating a complex terrain of resources, resistance and pedagogical knowledge constraints. Yet, rather than viewing these challenges as insurmountable barriers, they can be approached as opportunities for strategic innovation and advocacy. These challenges often manifest as tensions between competing priorities. For example, some schools may address time constraints by incorporating explicit skills instruction within the context of diverse texts, while others may create flexible scheduling that protects both instructional time and independent reading opportunities. Resource constraints, as experienced by

Keyan in his "constant trying to locate literature that highlights differences in culture," require creative solutions that maximise available resources while simultaneously developing advocacy for additional support. The establishment of resource-sharing networks among schools, strategic pursuit of targeted grant funding and judicious use of digital resources can significantly expand access to diverse materials even within tightly constrained budgets.

Resistance to change and pedagogical challenges often intertwine when implementing approaches that challenge traditional practices or address issues of diversity and equity. Such resistance—whether from colleagues, families or community members—necessitates a multifaceted response grounded in research evidence about the benefits of equitable literacy instruction for all children. The transformative outcomes documented in the vignettes, from increased student engagement to improved academic confidence, provide compelling evidence of the potential for the MELLE's impact on children's learning and development. These narratives serve not merely as inspirational anecdotes but also as powerful tools for advocacy and professional learning. As Kate demonstrated in her work with Aboriginal students, effective implementation does not require educators to possess comprehensive expertise across all cultures, but rather to adopt an epistemological stance as co-learners who value students' cultural knowledge. Rather than expecting individual teachers to master all dimensions simultaneously, successful schools can create teams that combine different areas of expertise. This approach reflects principles articulated in Freire's (2000) examination of dialogic education, wherein knowledge is conceptualised as emerging through reciprocal exchange between educators and learners, rather than through transmission models that position teachers as exclusive repositories of knowledge. By recognising and building upon existing strengths in teachers' practice, schools can implement iterative cycles of implementation, reflection and refinement that gradually build systemic capacity for culturally responsive literacy instruction while addressing both pedagogical limitations and resistance to change.

Policy constraints at various levels further complicate implementation, creating structural barriers that often reinforce existing inequities. These constraints—particularly regarding curriculum requirements, standardised assessment practices and resource allocation—require strategic navigation rather than passive acceptance. By identifying flexibility within existing frameworks, educators can create spaces for innovation even within seemingly rigid policy environments. Collaborative advocacy among colleagues and across institutions amplifies individual voices, creating collective pressure for policy reforms that better support equitable literacy education. Schools navigating assessment pressures can successfully develop complementary approaches that document growth across all dimensions of the MELLE framework. While meeting external accountability requirements, they can gather evidence of students' reading engagement, exposure to diverse texts, and development as critical readers. Perhaps most importantly, systematic documentation of implementation impact provides powerful evidence for policy advocacy, demonstrating the concrete benefits of approaches that integrate quality instruction, opportunity and representation. This evidence-based advocacy creates pathways towards more supportive policy environments while simultaneously addressing existing constraints. When viewed this way, implementation challenges become not just obstacles to overcome but also catalysts for transformative change within and beyond individual classrooms.

Integration Through Intentional Practice

The MELLE represents an opportunity for a paradigm shift in literacy education—one that moves beyond false dichotomies to recognise the complex, interconnected factors that shape children's literacy development. By integrating quality instruction, opportunity and representation within responsive cultural, community, curricular and contextual environments, this model offers a comprehensive approach to creating more equitable and effective literacy learning for all children. Implementing the MELLE requires sustained commitment and intentional practice through strategic planning, resource allocation and professional development. The vignettes presented confirm that such implementation is both possible and transformative across diverse educational contexts, even when navigating resource limitations, policy requirements and varied school environments. Strategic opportunities for integration exist within current educational systems, allowing educators to create literacy environments where all children develop as confident, engaged, and critical readers.

Conclusion: A New Paradigm for Reading Education

The Model for Equitable Literacy Learning Environments (MELLE) presented in this chapter offers a comprehensive model that can transform how literacy education can be conceptualised and practised. Through the integration of the three core dimensions—quality instruction, opportunity and representation—within responsive contextual environments, pathways can be created for all children to develop as capable, engaged readers. The vignettes shared throughout this chapter demonstrate the transformative potential of this integrated approach. The Sikh student who found his voice when his cultural identity was validated through literature; the Aboriginal students who became knowledge-leaders when given opportunities to share their cultural heritage; and the struggling readers who discovered newfound enthusiasm when presented with texts that reflected their lived experiences—these examples illustrate what becomes possible when educational environments honour both the technical aspects of literacy development and the sociocultural contexts in which reading occurs.

What distinguishes the MELLE from other educational frameworks is its underlying premise which refuses false dichotomies that have long characterised literacy debates. Instead of positioning evidence-based practice in opposition to cultural responsiveness, or academic achievement against identity affirmation, this model recognises these as complementary, mutually reinforcing aspects of comprehensive literacy education. When children receive quality instruction that builds on their cultural knowledge, have ample opportunities to engage with diverse texts, and see themselves and others authentically represented in what they read, they develop not only as skilled readers but also as confident, critical thinkers who recognise the power of literacy in their lives. The classroom examples presented in this chapter illustrate that implementing this model is both possible and powerful, even within the constraints of current educational systems.

The next chapter explores a detailed case study of culturally responsive literacy in action, providing an extended example of how the principles of the MELLE manifest in authentic classroom practice. This exemplar further illustrates how theoretical principles translate into transformative learning experiences that serve the needs of all children while addressing systemic inequities in literacy education.

Notes

1 Adam Goodes and Cathy Freeman are both well-known Aboriginal athletes. Both have spoken out bravely against discrimination and racism directed at themselves and others and are strong advocates for equity and inclusion. Both are former recipients of the Australian of the Year award.
2 Co-led by Gloria Boutte, Susi Long (now retired), Kamania Wynter-Hoyte, Janice Baines and Meir Muller.

References

Allington, R. L. (2014). How reading volume affects both reading fluency and reading achievement. *International Electronic Journal of Elementary Education*, 7(1), 13–26.

Australian Curriculum and Reporting Authority. (2025, May 19). New resources for teachers to support Australian students in understanding media literacy https://www.acara.edu.au/docs/default-source/media-releases/media-release-new-resource-for-teachers-to-support-australian-students-in-understanding-media-literacy-19-05-25.pdf?sfvrsn=13345307_2

Bus, A. G., Shang, Y., & Roskos, K. (2024). Building a stronger case for independent reading at school. *AERA Open*, 10, 1–17. https://doi.org/10.1177/23328584241267843

Cremin, T., Mottram, M., Powell, S., Collins, R., & Safford, K. (2014). *Building Communities of Engaged Readers: Reading for Pleasure*. Routledge.

Cremin, T., & Scholes, L. (2024). Reading for pleasure: Scrutinising the evidence base: Benefits, tensions and recommendations. *Language and Education*, 38(4), 537–559. https://doi.org/10.1080/09500782.2024.2324948

Dobrescu, I., Holden, R. J., Motta, A., Piccoli, A., Roberts, P., & Walker, S. (2022). Cultural context in standardized tests. *UNSW Economics Working Paper*, 2021–08. https://doi.org/10.2139/ssrn.3983663

Duke, N. K., Ward, A. E., & Pearson, P. D. (2021). The science of reading comprehension instruction. *The Reading Teacher*, 74(6), 663–672. https://doi.org/10.1002/trtr.1993

First Book Research & Insights. (2023). *The Impact of a Diverse Classroom Library*. First Book.

Freire, P. (2000). *Pedagogy of the Oppressed* (30th anniversary ed.). Continuum.

General Teaching Council for Scotland. (2019). *Guidelines for Accreditation of Initial Teacher Education Programmes in Scotland*. The General Teaching Council for Scotland.

General Teaching Council for Scotland. (2021). *The Standard for Provisional Registration: Mandatory Requirements for Registration with the General Teaching Council for Scotland*. The General Teaching Council for Scotland.

Jackson-Barrett, E. M., & Lee-Hammond, L. (2019). From Pink Floyd to Pink Hill: Transforming education from the bricks in the wall to the connections of Country in remote Aboriginal education. *Australian Journal of Teacher Education*, 44(10), 35–51.

McGeown, S., & Conradi Smith, K. (2024). Reading engagement matters! A new scale to measure and support children's engagement with books. *The Reading Teacher*, 77(4), 462–472. https://doi.org/10.1002/trtr.2267

Merke, S., Ganushcak, L., & van Steensel, R. (2024). Effects of additions to independent silent reading on students' reading proficiency, motivation, and behavior: Results of a meta-analysis. *Educational Research Review, 42*, 1–23 https://doi.org/10.1016/j.edurev.2023.100572

Muhammad, I., & Ali, S. K. (2019). *The Proudest Blue: A Story of Hijab and Family*. Andersen Press Ltd.

Nixon, J., & Fairclough, C. (2008). *I Am a Sikh*. Franklin Watts.

Stuart, S. (2020). *My Shadow Is Pink*. Larrikin House.

Stuart, S. (2022). *My Shadow Is Purple*. Larrikin House.

University of South Carolina. (2023). *Urban Education Cohort*. College of Education. https://www.sc.edu/study/colleges_schools/education/study/early_childhood_education/urban_education_cohort/index.php

Wright, T. S., Cabell, S. Q., Duke, N. K., & Souto-Manning, M. (2022). *Literacy Learning for Infants, Toddlers, & Preschoolers: Key Practices for Educators*. National Association for the Education of Young Children.

Culturally Responsive Literacy in Action

An Exemplar of Practice

Mikayla King and Helen Adam

8

Mikayla King is a Kalkadoon and Dutch Early Childhood Specialist at Department of Education, Western Australia, and Edith Cowan University, on sovereign Whadjuk land. She is a current PhD candidate in the ARC project, *Culturally Responsive Schooling*. Her teaching and research experience includes curriculum studies, Aboriginal epistemologies, Culturally Responsive Pedagogy and affect.

Introduction

The previous chapter presented the Model for Equitable Literacy Environments (MELLE) as a framework for creating more inclusive and effective literacy instruction through the integration of quality instruction, opportunity and representation within broader cultural, community, contextual and curricular dimensions. While theoretical frameworks provide valuable conceptual tools, seeing theory translated into authentic classroom practice offers deeper insights into how such models can transform literacy education.

This chapter presents an extended exemplar from Mikayla King, a Kalkadoon[1] teacher working with Year 4/5 students in a school in Perth, which includes a high enrolment of Noongar[2] children. This powerful narrative demonstrates how culturally responsive literacy instruction can engage students with complex concepts while affirming their cultural identities and positioning them as knowledge-holders and experts. Mikayla's thoughtful approach to resource selection, instructional design, and student engagement, sees the dimensions of the MELLE framework brought to life in a meaningful, contextually responsive way.

As you read this exemplar, consider how each element of the MELLE is embodied in Mikayla's practice—from the careful selection of texts that authentically represent Indigenous perspectives to the creation of opportunities for students to engage with multiple literacy modes to the quality instruction that scaffolds learning while honouring students' existing knowledge. Note also how the broader contexts of culture, community, school context and curriculum shape and inform Mikayla's decisions throughout this learning journey.

Following the exemplar, is an analysis of how this practice illuminates key aspects of the MELLE framework and discussing implications for educators seeking to implement similar approaches in their own contexts.

A Fishing Practice Inquiry: Working Through Indigenous STEM Knowledges and Literacy

A Narrative Shared by a Kalkadoon Teacher Working in Western Australia

I am a Kalkadoon teacher who is deeply engaged in the community and in the broader education profession. An important pedagogical practice for me is how I connect children to the world around us, in a historical and contemporary sense. I am going to share one of the ways I have done this recently and the importance of working with resources.

During the Perth Festival 2025 season, I visited an art installation called Karla Bidi, Fire Trail. Karla Bidi was a demonstration of the places in which Noongar peoples have gathered along the Swan River for thousands and thousands of years. One evening, my partner and I visited Warndoolier, Mardalup Park—a place we visit frequently as we travel to watch the football at Optus Stadium, across the river. During this visit, we learnt about the importance of Warndoolier as a popular fishing area—where Noongar peoples made fish traps through their sophisticated knowledges of Science, Design, Technology and Maths. I shared some photographs the following day with my Year 4/5 class with a high enrolment of Noongar children. There was great excitement generated in the room that day: children were excited as they had been to Warndoolier before; they knew information about Warndoolier from their families; and they became teachers and inquirers as part of this conversation. We followed this discussion with a video about the fish traps located in the river. This provocation directed the next eight weeks of our Technology and Science programme strongly infused with literacy learning.

As a Kalkadoon teacher, I have an insight into cultural knowledges from my own families and experiences of fishing. However, I am also aware that the knowledges involved in the development of a fish trap are sophisticated, complex and beyond my scope of knowledge. I felt a responsibility to honour the intellectualism of Noongar peoples and Aboriginal and Torres Strait Islander peoples nation-wide within this programme. To do this, I positioned students as researchers as we began by exploring our own families' historical and contemporary fishing practices. Students drew and narrated fishing roads on the jetty, hand lines on a low tide and spears in shallow water with family. Each story recalling information about community needs, the resources available to them and how much they needed to catch within a period of time. Each narrative recalling brief snippets of mathematical, scientific and technological processes. I wanted to demonstrate the intellectualism of Aboriginal and Torres Strait Islander peoples as the oldest scientists, engineers and mathematicians in the world through Aboriginal and Torres Strait Islander voices themselves. The story that has been historically denied to Australian children or told from an observer's perspective, which doesn't provide an insight into the richness of this practice. To do this, I began looking for resources.

It was important to me that I found high-quality resources. I began by looking for Aboriginal and/or Torres Strait Islander peoples who had authored resources relating directly to fishing practices or fish traps. This allowed us to understand the thought processes and the influence of community needs in the planning and construction phases. I then examined how Aboriginal and Torres Strait Islander peoples were represented; I specifically looked for strengths-based language, appropriate terminology, pictorial representations, recognition of the thousands of years of fishing practices and knowledge, and discussion of practices as both historical and contemporary—and not as a practice that died with the disruption of colonisation. This allowed students to see themselves as capable, competent peoples who come from a long line of fishing experts. As students were not familiar with the diversity in design of fish traps, I then began looking for visual representations through books, videos, artefacts and artworks. This allowed us to really understand how the use of resources was dependent on the geographical location where you lived and the purpose of the fish trap. It allowed us to understand the strong sense of sustainability as we witnessed the

Brewarrina Aboriginal Fish Traps (Pascoe, 2019) which are thousands of years old and identify differences in design due to natural resources and characteristics of particular locations. I then considered the purpose of the resources: Was I wanting one resource to communicate all of this, or many? It was important that we were able to access many resources as this enabled us to understand the diversity in knowledge and access a range of perspectives across Aboriginal and Torres Strait Islander communities. Finally, I then considered what scaffolding was required for children to access this resource. By access, I mean: Can children use their current knowledge, languages and experiences to understand the new conceptual ideas provided by the resources?

I found a range of resources that I used throughout this programme, including:

- Books: The First Scientists by Corey Tutt (2021), Young Dark Emu by Bruce Pascoe (2019), Design & Building on Country by Alison Page and Memmott (2024)
- Artefacts: variations of my own woven practices using both raffia and Yanjet, a river reed that grows along water systems on Noongar Country
- Videos: Indigenous Fish Traps by Menang Man—Harley Coyne (2015)
- Insights from Boola Bardip, the Western Australian Museum, about Booryulup, evidence of fish traps located in the Canning River.

Through the engagement of these resources, all children developed a very sophisticated understanding of fish traps and the fishing practices of Aboriginal and Torres Strait Islander peoples. There was a variety of teacher read-aloud, peer reading and silent reading of the resources. Each time, our purpose was to identify the main ideas within the resource and points of difference across geographical locations. In particular, these included the influence of community needs, sustainability and natural resources and how these impacted the design. I also used this opportunity to discuss ways that knowledge is communicated and shared, especially through the use of artworks and artefacts by Aboriginal and Torres Strait Islander peoples. At the end, children were able to use drawing and also verbal and written communication to explain complex scientific, mathematical and technological understandings that derived from the resources I identified above. At times, I found it hard to find the right resource as there are not many resources available about Noongar, specifically Whadjuk[3] fish traps. This influenced my decision to look more broadly towards the fishing practices of Aboriginal and Torres Strait Islander peoples nationally. There were some simplified versions of Aboriginal and Torres Strait Islander knowledges that I identified, but I was unwilling to compromise on quality or depth. At the same time, I came across resources that used technological vocabulary to discuss complex systems beyond our scope. I chose to talk through those and leave them in the *classroom library for children to look at in order to consolidate their understanding of technical terms through the combination of text and illustrations. In the final week of this program, a student brought in a book from home which identified Wiradjuri[4] fishing practices. She was so excited to show me and later that morning, she shared her findings with her peers.*

Overall, the most beneficial element of this whole process has been the shift in confidence, pride, ownership and ongoing commitment to the education of the Noongar student cohort. I believe this comes from seeing yourself represented in particular ways—seeing people in your community as the experts, seeing knowledges from your community as really important, being able to contribute to the conversations through experiences you bring from home and from knowing that you come from the oldest living mathematicians, scientists and engineers in the world.

I would like to acknowledge Nan Vivienne Hansen, Ilona McGuire, Jacob Nash, Chloe Ogilvie, Ian Wilkes, Nigel Wilkes, Alta Winmar and the Perth Festival Noongar advisory circle for their contributions and generosity in sharing cultural knowledges that enabled Karla Bidi.

Analysis: The MELLE Framework in Action

This exemplar powerfully illustrates how the three core dimensions of the Model for Equitable Literacy Environments (MELLE) can be integrated to create transformative learning experiences. The sections below examine each dimension as evidenced in Mikayla's practice.

Quality Instruction

Mikayla's approach to instruction exemplifies several key principles of quality teaching within a culturally responsive framework:

- **Scaffolded learning**: Mikayla thoughtfully sequenced learning experiences, beginning with students' personal connections to fishing practices before expanding to broader Indigenous knowledge systems. This gradual building of understanding allowed students to connect new knowledge to their existing experiences.
- **Purpose-driven literacy**: Reading, writing speaking, and viewing were embedded within meaningful inquiry rather than taught as isolated skills. Mikayla notes that "each time, our purpose was to identify the

main ideas within the resource and points of difference across geographical locations." This intentional focus gave students authentic reasons to engage with texts.

Multi-modal approaches: Mikayla integrated multiple literacy modes, including visual (photographs, videos, artefacts), oral (discussions, narratives) and written (books, student explanations) communication. This multi-modal approach honoured diverse ways of knowing and expressing understanding.

Cross-curricular integration: Literacy was seamlessly woven into Science and Technology, demonstrating how reading and communicating are essential tools across all learning areas. This integration reflects best practice in literacy education.

Metacognitive awareness: Mikayla explicitly discussed "ways that knowledge is communicated and shared," helping students develop awareness of how different texts and artefacts convey meaning—a sophisticated literacy understanding.

Opportunity

Mikayla created rich opportunities for students to engage with diverse texts and literacy practices:

Access to high-quality texts: Mikayla's careful curation of resources by Indigenous authors and creators provided students with opportunities to engage with authentic voices and perspectives. Despite challenges in finding specific local resources, Mikayla refused to "compromise on quality or depth."

Multiple entry points: By providing resources in various formats—books, videos, artefacts, museum insights— Mikayla ensured that all students could access the content through modes that matched their learning preferences and strengths.

Extended engagement: The eight-week duration of the project allowed for deep exploration rather than superficial coverage, providing sustained opportunity for students to develop sophisticated understanding of the cultural and technological knowledge and skills, as well as the comprehension and creation of a range of text types and artefacts of learning.

Student agency: Students were positioned as researchers and knowledge-sharers, with opportunities to contribute their own family and cultural knowledge and, as in the case of the student who brought in a book about Wiradjuri fishing practices, to extend the classroom resources.

Classroom environment: Mikayla created an environment where resources were available for students to explore independently, noting that they left more advanced texts "in the classroom library for children to look at in order to consolidate their understanding of technical terms through the combination of text and illustrations," thus providing opportunities for self-directed learning.

Representation

The dimension of representation is perhaps most powerfully exemplified in this narrative:

Authentic Indigenous voices: Mikayla prioritised resources created by Aboriginal and Torres Strait Islander authors and knowledge-holders, ensuring authentic representation rather than outsider perspectives.

Strengths-based portrayal: Mikayla explicitly sought resources with "strengths-based language, appropriate terminology, pictorial representations, recognition of the thousands of years of fishing practices and knowledge, and discussion of practices as both historical and contemporary." This criterion demonstrates a sophisticated understanding of what constitutes respectful representation.

Local and broader perspectives: By connecting local Noongar knowledge with broader Indigenous knowledge systems, Mikayla helped students see their cultural heritage within a national context while maintaining the specificity of local traditions.

Contemporary relevance: Mikayla deliberately sought resources that depicted Indigenous knowledge as living and continuing, rather than as historical curiosities, thereby challenging the colonial narrative that such practices "died with the disruption of colonisation." As noted by Pascoe (2019), "They [British officers and convicts] planned to clear land, grow crops, farm, build houses, make towns and cities and establish law and order as they recognised it. In their rush for possession of land, they turned their eyes away from the obvious signs of the civilisation that already existed" (p. 9). As a result, there is a responsibility to teach the knowledges that have survived attempted erasure.

Multiple perspectives: By using various resources, Mikayla enabled students to "understand the diversity in knowledge and access a range of perspectives across Aboriginal and Torres Strait Islander communities," avoiding the pitfall of presenting Indigenous cultures as monolithic.

The Contextual Dimensions

The exemplar also powerfully demonstrates how the broader contexts of culture, community, educational setting and curriculum shaped the implementation of the three core dimensions:

Culture/s: Mikayla navigated complex cultural terrain with remarkable sensitivity. As a Kalkadoon teacher working with predominantly Noongar students, she demonstrated respect for specific local knowledge while acknowledging her own cultural perspective and limitations: "I have an insight into cultural knowledges from my own families and experiences of fishing, however, I am also aware that the knowledges involved in the development of a fish trap are sophisticated, complex and beyond my scope of knowledge." This transparency models cultural humility while still leveraging Mikayla's Indigenous perspective.

Community: The learning journey began with a local connection—Mikayla's visit to *Warndoolier*/Mardalup Park during a cultural festival—and expanded to incorporate both family knowledge and broader Indigenous perspectives. By validating students' existing knowledge about local places and inviting them to share family fishing practices, Mikayla created meaningful links between home and school literacy. The acknowledgment of community experts at the end of the narrative further demonstrates both involvement of, and respect for, community knowledge-holders.

Context: Mikayla tailored her approach to the specific school and classroom context, with its "high enrolment of Noongar children," recognising the opportunity to affirm these students' cultural identities while engaging all students in meaningful learning. The grade level (Year 4/5) was considered in the selection and scaffolding of resources, with Mikayla noting that some materials contained "technological vocabulary to discuss complex systems beyond our scope."

Curriculum: Rather than forcing cultural content into predetermined curriculum boundaries, Mikayla allowed student interest to drive an integrated eight-week Science and Technology programme. This responsive approach to curriculum demonstrates how quality literacy instruction can emerge organically from student engagement with culturally relevant content, while still addressing key learning areas, skills and curriculum content.

Transformative Outcomes: Beyond Academic Achievement

What makes this exemplar particularly powerful is the evidence of transformative impact on students. Mikayla notes that "the most beneficial element of this whole process has been the shift in confidence, pride, ownership and commitment to education of the Noongar student cohort." This observation aligns with research on culturally responsive pedagogy, which suggests that when students see themselves and their communities represented in affirming ways, they develop stronger academic identities and engagement.

The specific elements Mikayla identifies as contributing to this transformation are worth highlighting:

1. "Seeing people in your community as the experts"
2. "Seeing knowledges from your community as really important"
3. "Being able to contribute to the conversations through experiences you bring from home"
4. "Knowing that you come from the oldest living mathematicians, scientists and engineers in the world"

These four elements connect directly to the dimensions of the MELLE: representation (seeing community members as experts), quality instruction (valuing Indigenous knowledge as sophisticated and important), opportunity (creating spaces for students to contribute their home experiences) and cultural context (positioning Indigenous knowledge within a global historical perspective).

The fact that a student was motivated to bring in a book from home about Wiradjuri fishing practices—and was "so excited" to share it with peers—provides additional evidence of the program's impact on student engagement and motivation. This student moved beyond being a passive recipient of knowledge to actively extending the class's learning resources, demonstrating ownership of the learning process.

Implications for Practice

This exemplar offers several important insights for educators seeking to implement the MELLE framework in their own contexts:

Resource Selection Criteria

Mikayla's detailed explanation of criteria for selecting appropriate resources provides valuable guidance:

1. **Authentic authorship**: Prioritising resources created by members of the represented cultural groups
2. **Strengths-based representation**: Looking for language and imagery that depicts the group in empowering ways
3. **Historical accuracy and continuity**: Ensuring resources acknowledge both historical significance and contemporary relevance
4. **Visual and multi-modal components**: Providing multiple ways to access and understand the content
5. **Multiple sources**: Using various resources to present diverse perspectives within cultural groups
6. **Accessibility**: Considering how to scaffold resources for specific student populations

This approach adopted by Mikayla for resource evaluation could be applied across diverse cultural contexts and subject areas.

Positioning Students as Knowledge-Holders

A key aspect of Mikayla's approach was positioning students as researchers and experts rather than passive recipients of information. By inviting students to share their family knowledge and community connections, Mikayla created a more equitable knowledge exchange in the classroom. This approach aligns with culturally responsive pedagogies that recognise and build upon students' "funds of knowledge" (Moll et al., 1992).

Cross-Curricular Integration of Literacy

The exemplar demonstrates how literacy can be seamlessly integrated across curriculum areas, with reading, writing, speaking and viewing embedded within Science and Technology learning. This approach reflects best practice in literacy education, which recognises that literacy skills are most effectively developed when used for authentic purposes across the curriculum.

Teacher Positionality and Cultural Humility

Mikayla's acknowledgment of their own cultural perspective and limitations offers an important model of cultural humility. While Mikayla's Kalkadoon identity provided some insights into Indigenous knowledge systems, she recognised the specificity of Noongar knowledge and did not position herself as an expert in all Indigenous perspectives. This approach demonstrates how teachers can respectfully engage with cultural content, even when it is not from their own cultural background. This is especially important for many teachers from Anglo-Eurocentric backgrounds that make up the majority of the teaching workforce. As outlined in Chapter 5, my research, and that of others, has shown many teachers avoid addressing diversity and cultural knowledge due to a lack of confidence, while others reinforce outdated and stereotypical notions of culture through failing to recognise their own limited knowledge.

Conclusion

This exemplar powerfully demonstrates the transformative potential of the MELLE when implemented with thoughtfulness, cultural sensitivity and pedagogical skill. Mikayla's approach integrates quality instruction, opportunity and representation within responsive cultural, community, school and curricular contexts to create a learning sequence that not only developed students' literacy and content knowledge but also affirmed their cultural identities and positioned them as knowledge-holders.

The outcomes described—increased confidence, pride, ownership and commitment to education—illustrate the profound impact that culturally responsive literacy instruction can have, particularly for students from historically marginalised communities. By seeing themselves, their communities and their knowledge systems represented in affirming ways, these students developed stronger connections to both their cultural heritage and their educational journey. For students who identified with other Aboriginal language groups, and for those not from Aboriginal backgrounds, this engagement provided opportunities for strengthening understandings of the rich, complex and sophisticated processes of Aboriginal and Torres Strait Islander knowledges on the Country Australians live and grow on.

As the educational community strives to create more equitable literacy environments for all children, exemplars like this provide both inspiration and practical guidance. They demonstrate that creating such environments is not simply about following a prescribed formula but about responding thoughtfully to the specific contexts, needs and strengths of students and communities. Most importantly, they demonstrate that when quality instruction, opportunity and representation are infused within responsive contexts, conditions are created for all students to thrive as readers, writers, thinkers and community members.

Notes

1 Kalkadoon (**Kalkatungu**) are an Indigenous Australian language group from the Mount Isa region of Queensland. https://www.kalkadoonpbc.com.au/about-us/who-we-are.
2 Noongar means 'a person of the south-west of Western Australia,' or the name for the 'original inhabitants of the south-west of Western Australia'. https://www.noongarculture.org.au/noongar/.
3 Whadjuk is the name of the dialectal group from the Perth area. *Whadjuk* is situated south of *Yued* and north of the *Pinjarup* dialectal groups. https://www.noongarculture.org.au/whadjuk/.
4 The Wiradjuri people are the traditional landowners of Peak Hill, which is located in Central West New South Wales. https://australian.museum/learn/cultures/atsi-collection/australian-archaeology/indigenous-objects-peak-hill-nsw/.

References

Coyne, H. (2015, July 15). Fishing the old way: Indigenous Fish Traps of Western Australia [video]. https://www.youtube.com/watch?v=qma1MC1_PAs

Moll, L. C., Amanti, C., Neff, D., & Gonzalez, N. (1992). Funds of knowledge for teaching: Using a qualitative approach to connect homes and classrooms. *Theory Into Practice*, *31*(2), 132–141.

Page, A., & Memmott, P. (2024). *Design and Building on Country: First Knowledges for Younger Readers*. Thames & Hudson Australia Pty, Limited.

Pascoe, B. (2019). *Young Dark Emu: A Truer History*. Magabala Books.

Tutt, C. (2021). *The First Scientists: Deadly Inventions and Innovations from Australia's First Peoples*. Hardie Grant Explore.

Policy and Practice 9

Introduction: Establishing the Policy Context for Literacy Education

The previous chapters have explored the complex interplay between quality instruction, opportunity to read and representation, with Chapter 7 presenting the Model for Equitable Literacy Learning Environments (MELLE) that centres this interplay as essential for truly equitable education. This chapter examines how these components function within broader educational policy landscapes and institutional structures, considering both constraints of existing systems and possibilities for transformation.

Educational policies, particularly those influenced by ongoing debates about reading instruction, have profoundly shaped classroom practices. Despite often being prefaced on claims of social justice, these frequently result in unintended consequences for children from traditionally marginalised backgrounds. These policy challenges are not unique to Australia but are evident across many English-speaking countries. Examining these relationships critically is necessary to identify pathways towards more equitable literacy education for all children. Educational policy does not exist in a vacuum but rather emerges from complex historical, political and social contexts. The arguments about reading instruction dominating literacy policy discussions reflect not only disagreements about effective instruction but also competing visions of education's purpose and the role of schools in society. These debates have influenced policy decisions, curriculum development, resource allocation and assessment practices, creating a landscape that educators must navigate daily in their efforts to serve all children equitably.

DOI: 10.4324/9781003628217-9

Theoretical Framework: Policy Mobilities, Enactment and Practice Architectures

Understanding the relationship between policy and practice in literacy education requires theoretical perspectives that illuminate how policies move, transform and are enacted across different contexts. Three interrelated theoretical perspectives are particularly useful for analysing how literacy policies operate across multiple levels and contexts:

Policy mobilities research provides insights into how literacy policy ideas travel between spaces and are reassembled in specific contexts. Ball (2016) argues that policies are mobile not in distinct forms but rather in a piecemeal fashion, being "(re)assembled in particular ways, in particular places, and for particular purposes" (p. 549). These policies move through networks of 'actors'—including politicians, bureaucrats, edu-businesses, philanthropists and consultants—who establish policy legitimacy across different contexts. The influence of phonics screening checks originally developed in England but now adopted in most states of Australia demonstrates how specific literacy assessment tools can travel through these networks of influence (Ellis & Moss, 2014).

The concept of **policy enactment** moves beyond simplistic notions of implementation to recognise that policies are actively interpreted, translated and reconstructed by various stakeholders at different levels of educational systems. Braun et al. (2011) argue that as policies move from national frameworks to classroom practice, they undergo multiple transformations, with teachers not simply implementing policy directives but actively making sense of them within their specific contexts. This enactment perspective helps explain the gap between policy intentions and classroom realities—even when policy documents explicitly promote equity and inclusion, the ways they are enacted in practice may reinforce rather than challenge existing inequities (Singh et al., 2014).

Complementing these perspectives, Wilkins and Gobby's (2024) research on the **governmentality approach** to education governance reveals how risk functions as a rationality for recalibrating education policy through frameworks of calculation and control. Particularly significant for understanding literacy policy is their analysis of how children from marginalised backgrounds become constructed as 'risk subjects' requiring management and intervention. Building on sociological critiques of risk in education (Hardy, 2015; Lubeck & Garrett, 1990; Ratner, 2019), Wilkins and Gobby demonstrate how "certain children and young people are represented as particular kinds of risk subjects and in turn constituted as 'risk objects' to be actively managed" (Wilkins & Gobby, 2024, p. 924). This perspective reveals the troubling ways in which children from Indigenous, culturally and racially marginalised, and economically disadvantaged backgrounds become positioned as deficient subjects who "lack certain social, psychological or intellectual utilities" or "fail to utilise their decision making in rationally and morally superior ways" (Wilkins & Gobby, 2024, p. 925).

Such deficit framings directly contradict the asset-based approaches advocated throughout this book, particularly in Chapter 3's critique of deficit perspectives in reading instruction. When literacy policies construct children as 'at risk' due to perceived lacks or deficiencies, they obscure the rich linguistic and cultural resources these children bring to their learning—the very 'funds of knowledge' that culturally responsive pedagogy seeks to recognise and build upon. This risk-based rationality creates what Wilkins and Gobby term "new forms of responsibility and self-governing centred around 'prudentialism and calculation'", whereby educational institutions focus on managing and containing perceived deficits rather than creating the kinds of affirming, culturally responsive literacy environments centred in the MELLE.

The Journey of Reading Policy: From Global Influences to Classroom Practice

In the early 2000s, three major reports fundamentally reshaped literacy education policy across English-speaking countries: the National Inquiry into the Teaching of Literacy in Australia (2005); the National Reading Panel in the United States (2000); and the Rose Review in the United Kingdom (2006). These reports emerged during a period of increasing focus on educational accountability and standardisation, with their emphasis on evidence-based practices aligning with broader neoliberal educational reforms that privileged measurable outcomes and standardised approaches (Lingard, 2010; Sahlberg, 2011). While the reports themselves offered nuanced recommendations about systematic and explicit phonics instruction within broader, integrated approaches to literacy, their interpretation through multiple policy layers has often narrowed to rigid mandates that emphasise discrete skills at the expense of other important dimensions of literacy development (Ellis & Moss, 2014).

The translation of these influential reports through multiple layers—from national policy to state/regional frameworks, district implementation, school leadership and, finally, classroom practice—has created significant tensions within educational systems. This journey from research to classroom implementation illustrates what Ball (2016) describes as policy enactment—the complex process through which policies are interpreted, translated and put into practice by various stakeholders. At each stage of translation, the original research findings often become simplified and distilled into more structured approaches that may not fully capture the nuance and context of the original research. This simplification can sometimes lead to an overemphasis on technical aspects of reading (such as decoding and phonological awareness) without due attention to meaning-making, critical literacy and reading engagement—all essential components of comprehensive literacy development, along with the technical aspects of reading.

The specific ways in which policy ideas are translated and enacted vary across contexts based on existing structures, resources and local priorities. In Australia, this policy trajectory has had particular implications for resource distribution. Rorris (2023) documents how funding policies have systematically privileged non-government schools while failing to adequately resource public schools which serve the majority of students from disadvantaged backgrounds. This policy trajectory demonstrates what Ball (2016) describes as "reassembling" of global policy trends in specific national contexts, with Australian interpretations of market-based education reforms creating distinct patterns of resource distribution that directly impact literacy provision.

Key Tensions in the Policy Landscape

The translation of literacy policies through multiple layers—from national frameworks to classroom practice—creates several key tensions that impact equitable education provision. These tensions emerge from broader contradictions within educational governance and highlight the challenges of developing genuinely inclusive literacy education within current policy paradigms.

Standardisation vs. Cultural Responsiveness

When policies are translated into practice, they often promote standardised approaches that fail to account for linguistic and cultural diversity among students. As discussed in Chapter 3, when evidence is interpreted through a narrow and monocultural lens, the resulting practices may disadvantage children whose language experiences differ from the dominant norm—reinforcing what Chapter 3 identified as raciolinguistic ideologies that position certain forms of language as deficient rather than different (Cushing, 2021; Flores & Rosa, 2015). This standardisation creates what Gorur (2016) describes as "seeing like PISA"—a reductionist view that focuses narrowly on measurable outcomes while overlooking the complex social and cultural dimensions of education. This standardisation epitomises what Gorur (2016) compares to 18th-century German scientific forestry practices. Gorur highlights how German foresters transformed diverse, complex forests into uniform rows of single-species trees to make them more countable, predictable and economically efficient. While initially successful, this standardisation ultimately depleted soil fertility and destroyed biodiversity. Similarly, contemporary education systems risk reducing complex literacy learning environments to standardised, measurable components that may appear orderly and efficient in the short term, but which undermine the rich diversity of knowledge and experiences essential for equitable literacy development—directly contradicting the integration of quality instruction, opportunity and representation at the heart of the MELLE framework.

This tension between standardisation and responsiveness is further evident in classroom implementation. Recent evidence from Comstock et al. (2023) demonstrates that teachers with strong cultural responsiveness self-efficacy are more likely to implement culturally responsive practices, yet the standardised policy approaches that emerge from "seeing like PISA" often fail to build this self-efficacy. Just as forest management practices that ignored ecological complexity led to depleted environments, educational policies that prioritise standardisation over teacher capacity for cultural responsiveness risk undermining the professional knowledge essential for equitable literacy instruction. Comstock and colleagues' findings suggest that professional learning which builds teacher self-efficacy for culturally responsive teaching may be critical to bridging the gap between standardisation and responsiveness, but such approaches are rarely centralised in policy mandates that focus primarily on measurable outcomes.

Further, many curriculum documents, such as the Australian Curriculum, explicitly value linguistic and cultural diversity through cross-curricular priorities and general capabilities that foreground intercultural understanding, ethical considerations and critical thinking. However, a significant mismatch often emerges between these stated intentions and their enactment in classrooms. This disconnect largely stems from competing policy priorities—particularly the increasing emphasis on standardised assessment and mandated instructional approaches. Gorur (2016) documents how measurement and comparison tools like NAPLAN and PISA create policy environments that privilege standardisation over responsiveness. When quality instruction becomes narrowly defined through high-stakes assessment frameworks and prescriptive methodologies, the space for the kind of culturally responsive teaching envisioned in curriculum documents becomes severely constrained.

Evidence vs. Experience

Another key tension exists in how 'evidence-based practice' is conceptualised and enacted. While policy documents increasingly emphasise evidence-based approaches, the definition of what constitutes valid evidence is often narrowly constrained, privileging certain research methodologies and outcomes over others. As Connolly (2017) argues, despite the increasing prominence of evidence-based practice in education policy - particularly through the use of randomised controlled trials- there remains significant disagreement about what constitutes 'good evidence' and whose perspectives are valued in determining evidence quality.

The 'gold standard' of evidence prioritised in many policy frameworks is the randomised controlled trial (RCT), which seeks to isolate the effects of specific interventions. Cartwright (2007, p. 11) provocatively questioned this designation, arguing that RCTs are 'both necessary and not sufficient' for establishing causal claims in complex social contexts. Recent analyses by Coldwell and Moore (2024) and Parra and Edwards (2024) have further illuminated these limitations, highlighting the difficulty of maintaining statistically comparable treatment and control groups over time due to attrition and human agency. RCTs necessarily standardise implementation to isolate effects, which can obscure how interventions interact with the cultural, linguistic and social contexts essential to literacy development in diverse communities (Parra & Edwards, 2024). Despite claims of objectivity, preference for experimental research might privilege certain types of knowledge production while potentially limiting broader approaches to educational reform (Coldwell & Moore, 2024). As Biesta (2010) argues, this narrow focus on what can be measured through experimental designs fails to address the normative and ethical dimensions of education that are essential to quality provision.

Comber and Woods (2018) highlight the importance of considering multiple forms of evidence, including classroom case studies, teacher action research and other forms of practice-based evidence. Their research demonstrates how teachers' contextual knowledge and responsive practice can generate important insights that experimental designs may miss. This expanded view of evidence recognises the complexity of literacy learning in diverse contexts and values both scientific and experiential knowledge. These tensions are particularly evident in how educational leaders navigate competing demands. School leaders who prioritise cultural responsiveness in professional learning help teachers develop the knowledge and skills needed to implement the kind of integrated approach central to the MELLE. Without this support, teachers may struggle to move beyond prescribed approaches often emphasised in policy documents and commercial programmes.

Autonomy vs. Accountability

The tensions between standardisation and cultural responsiveness reflect broader policy shifts in Australian education. MacDonald et al. (2021) provide a historical overview of school autonomy policies in Australian public education from the 1970s to the present, demonstrating how accountability measures have increasingly constrained genuine autonomy, particularly for schools serving disadvantaged communities. Similarly, Keddie et al. (2020) identify several paradoxes in school autonomy policies that can undermine social justice aims, including how market-driven approaches to education can limit rather than enhance equitable resource allocation.

Further, high-stakes literacy assessments linked to policy initiatives often drive instructional decisions, leading to a narrowed curriculum focused on measurable skills at the expense of broader literacy development. When schools and teachers are evaluated based on students' performance on standardised tests, there is strong pressure to focus instruction on the specific skills measured by these assessments. This assessment-driven approach can significantly reduce opportunities for the kind of rich, engaging literacy experiences described in Chapters 4 and 5. Time for reading for pleasure, exploration of diverse texts, and development of critical literacy may be sacrificed in favour of test preparation and skills practice. As Chapter 4 demonstrated, this trend directly contradicts research showing that reading volume and engagement with self-selected texts are crucial factors in literacy development—with research from Bus et al. (2024) and Cremin and Scholes (2024) confirming that independent reading opportunities enhance both reading attitudes and achievement. For children from marginalised backgrounds, this narrowing of the curriculum can be particularly damaging, as it reduces the likelihood that they will encounter texts that reflect their lives and experiences or develop the kind of positive relationship with reading that sustains lifelong literacy engagement.

These tensions between standardisation and cultural responsiveness, evidence and experience, and autonomy and accountability do not emerge in a vacuum but are underpinned by particular ways of conceptualising children and their educational needs. Understanding how these tensions manifest in practice requires examining the discursive mechanisms through which certain children become constructed as problems requiring policy intervention rather than as learners with valuable resources to contribute to their educational communities.

The Construction of 'At-Risk' Readers

The governmentality perspective illuminated by Wilkins and Gobby (2024) provides crucial insights into how literacy policies construct certain children as 'at-risk' readers requiring intervention and management. This construction process has profound implications for the three dimensions of the MELLE framework, as it shapes how quality instruction is conceived, which children receive opportunities to read, and whose experiences are represented in educational materials.

The discourse of 'at-risk' readers typically focuses on children who struggle with standardised assessments of reading skills, particularly those from Indigenous, culturally and racially marginalised, and economically disadvantaged backgrounds. However, as Wilkins and Gobby demonstrate, this classification process involves "deficit understandings of risk" that position children as lacking essential capabilities rather than recognising the systemic inequities that limit their educational opportunities. This deficit framing becomes particularly problematic when children are judged to be at risk "because they lack certain social, psychological or intellectual utilities" or because they are "subject to environments that impede their personal freedom or personal responsibility" (Wilkins & Gobby, 2024).

Such constructions fundamentally misrepresent the challenges many children face in literacy development. As Chapter 4 established, children from economically disadvantaged backgrounds often lack access to books and reading opportunities not because of personal deficiencies but because of systemic inequities in resource allocation. Similarly, Chapter 5 demonstrated that when children struggle to engage with reading materials, this often reflects the absence of authentic representation rather than individual inadequacies. The risk discourse, however, obscures these structural factors by focusing attention on managing individual children rather than transforming the conditions that create educational inequity.

The policy implications of this risk-based thinking are far-reaching. When children are constructed as risk objects requiring management, educational responses tend to emphasise remediation and intervention rather than the kind of strengths-based, culturally responsive approaches advocated in this book.

This creates what Wilkins and Gobby describe as "frameworks of calculation and control" that privilege narrow measures of reading proficiency whilst marginalising the broader dimensions of literacy development—including engagement, critical thinking and cultural connections—that are essential for creating truly equitable literacy environments.

Stakeholder Dynamics: The Ecology of Literacy Policy Implementation

As policy directives move from government frameworks to classroom practice, they pass through multiple layers of interpretation and implementation. This translation process involves three key stakeholder groups—policymakers, educational leaders and commercial publishers—each playing distinct but interconnected roles in shaping literacy education. The interactions between these stakeholders and their decisions create a policy environment that significantly impacts equity in literacy instruction.

Policymakers and System-Level Decisions

Policymakers at local, regional, state and national levels establish the frameworks, requirements and accountability systems that shape literacy education. While curriculum frameworks often explicitly promote equity and inclusion, the translation of these principles into practice is frequently compromised by other policy elements. Somewhat ironically, many mandated approaches to reading instruction are promoted on the premise of addressing equity, yet they primarily focus on standard English at the expense of the linguistic and cultural diversity discussed in earlier chapters. Wright et al. (2022) highlight how such approaches can undermine children's linguistic confidence and sense of belonging, contradicting the very equity principles expressed in curriculum frameworks. Cushing's (2021, 2023) research on language policies in English primary schools highlights how standard language ideology becomes embedded in school policies and commercial materials. His analysis of school policies reveals how many have adopted language that positions teachers as "standard language 'role models'" who have the authority to police, regulate and suppress students' language. This creates what he terms "policies of surveillance" where students' linguistic diversity is often framed as problematic rather than valuable. In addition, despite the clear need for targeted funding for diverse reading materials, professional development in culturally responsive pedagogy and additional support for schools serving marginalised communities, resource allocation frequently reinforces rather than addresses existing inequities. This pattern was evident across all the countries visited during my Churchill Fellowship, where schools serving disadvantaged communities often had fewer resources for libraries and literacy programmes than those in more affluent areas.

Schools and Educational Leaders

Schools and their leadership teams serve as critical mediators between policy directives and classroom practice. Their decisions regarding resource allocation, professional development and instructional priorities significantly impact how policies translate into classroom experiences for children. It is important to acknowledge that many educational leaders are deeply committed to equity and work tirelessly to create inclusive learning environments despite operating within significant structural and resource constraints. These leaders navigate complex policy landscapes, competing priorities and limited budgets while attempting to implement equitable practices. As Wilkinson et al. (2024) demonstrate in their research on 'enabling niches,' resourceful leaders often find creative ways to prioritise equity even within constraining policy environments. Their efforts, often unrecognised in broader policy discussions, represent crucial acts of resistance against standardising tendencies in educational policy.

Within these constraints, school-level decisions about which books to purchase, which programmes to implement and how to allocate instructional time all influence children's access to diverse reading materials and approaches. The professional learning opportunities provided to teachers reflect and reinforce particular views about reading instruction, potentially limiting or expanding teachers' exposure to diverse perspectives and approaches. Whitaker and Valtierra (2018) identify three key dispositional domains essential for culturally responsive teaching: Disposition for Praxis (teachers' commitment to self-awareness and improvement); Disposition for Community (valuing collaborative relationships); and Disposition for Social Justice (recognising schools as sites for challenging inequity). Their research suggests that school leaders play a crucial role in fostering these dispositions through the professional learning opportunities and organisational cultures they create. Many leaders actively seek to develop these dispositions despite systemic pressures that push towards standardisation and narrow accountability measures.

Publishers and the Commercial Landscape

Commercial publishers wield considerable influence in determining which texts and educational resources reach classrooms. The selection, development and marketing of reading materials reflect not only educational considerations but also commercial interests. Despite increasing calls for diverse representation, mainstream educational publishers continue to produce materials that predominantly represent white, middle-class experiences and perspectives. The data presented in Chapter 5 regarding the lack of diverse representation in award-winning children's books reflects broader publishing trends. This limited diversity in published materials means that many children never see themselves or their communities authentically represented in the books they encounter at school.

Publishers often develop materials designed to align with government policies and curriculum frameworks, reinforcing dominant approaches to reading instruction that may not serve all children equitably. The marketing of complete reading 'systems' or programmes encourages schools to adopt standardised approaches rather than developing contextually responsive literacy practices that draw on diverse texts and approaches. Economic factors also play a significant role in limiting access to diverse books. High-quality, culturally diverse books are often published by smaller, independent publishers and may be more expensive or less accessible than materials from major publishing houses, creating economic barriers to diversifying classroom libraries. For schools in low-socioeconomic areas, which often have more limited budgets, this can make it particularly difficult to build representative book collections. However, there are some promising developments in this landscape. Some publishers are actively working to increase representation in their texts, and organisations like First Book, We Need Diverse Books and the Indigenous Literacy Foundation are advocating for change within the publishing industry. Digital publishing has also created new opportunities for diverse voices to reach readers, potentially bypassing traditional gatekeepers.

The complex interactions between policymakers, educational leaders and publishers described above operate within broader political and social contexts that can either support or undermine efforts to create equitable literacy environments. Recent developments across English-speaking countries suggest that the challenges facing equitable literacy education are intensifying, creating new urgencies for the kind of integrated approach to quality instruction, opportunity and representation underpinning the MELLE. These emerging threats require careful analysis to understand how they intersect with, and amplify, the existing tensions and inequities documented throughout this book.

Current and Emerging Threats to Equitable Literacy Education

My Churchill Fellowship and other evidence in this book reveal several concerning threats to equitable literacy education that require urgent attention. These challenges are not unique to any one country but represent broader societal tensions that impact educational policy and practice.

The alarming rise in book censorship and challenges to diverse literature represents a significant threat to the representation dimension of the MELLE. As detailed in Chapter 5, books featuring protagonists of colour or LGBTQIA+ characters are disproportionately targeted in these campaigns. When diverse books are removed from libraries and classrooms, children lose access both to mirrors that reflect their own experiences and to windows into the experiences of others—the essential dimensions of representation that Bishop (1990) articulated and which Chapter 5 explored in depth. These movements threaten to turn back the clock on progress in diversifying children's literature and educational resources, creating environments where educators and librarians fear repercussions for providing diverse books and supporting inclusive education.

The recent political changes in the United States, with the return of a presidential administration advocating for more conservative educational policies, raise significant concerns for equitable literacy education globally. The previous term of this administration saw attempts to limit diversity initiatives in education, challenges to Critical Race Theory in curricula, and the promotion of 'patriotic education' approaches that often present simplified historical narratives. These policy directions have already begun to influence political agendas in other English-speaking countries, including Australia and the United Kingdom, where similar rhetorical challenges to culturally responsive education and diverse curricula have emerged. The transnational nature of these conservative educational movements, facilitated by shared media ecosystems and policy networks, poses challenges to the progress in culturally responsive pedagogy across Western democracies because such movements often challenge or undermine the principles of Culturally Responsive Pedagogy (CRP), which emphasises adapting teaching to meet the diverse cultural needs and backgrounds of students.

Throughout my Fellowship journey, poverty emerged as a critical factor limiting children's access to books and educational opportunities. As detailed in Chapter 4, children living in poverty often have limited or no access to books at home, and schools serving high-poverty communities frequently have fewer resources for classroom and school libraries. This inequitable distribution of resources compounds the challenges faced by children from underrepresented backgrounds, many of whom are disproportionately affected by poverty. When children lack access to books that reflect their experiences and identities, their motivation to read and sense of belonging in educational settings are compromised. These structural inequities are further exacerbated by systemic funding disparities between public and private education sectors in Australia. While some states have recently committed to implementing full Gonski (Gonski et al., 2018) funding recommendations (needs-based funding formulas designed to ensure adequate resources for all schools), current funding models have persistently disadvantaged public schools serving the majority of children from low socioeconomic backgrounds, Indigenous communities and culturally diverse populations (Rorris, 2023). This inequitable distribution of resources directly impacts the ability of affected schools to provide diverse reading materials and literacy supports to the children who need them most. These Australian patterns reflect broader international trends documented by UNESCO (2021), which found that funding mechanisms across many countries systematically advantage non-state actors while limiting resources for public institutions serving disadvantaged populations.

The Intensification of Risk-Based Governance

The risk-based rationalities identified by Wilkins and Gobby (2024) have intensified in recent literacy policy developments across English-speaking countries. This intensification manifests in several concerning ways that directly threaten the implementation of equitable literacy frameworks like the MELLE.

Increasingly, literacy policies frame children from marginalised backgrounds as subjects requiring intensive surveillance and management rather than as learners with valuable cultural and linguistic resources. This surveillance extends beyond academic performance to encompass family practices, home literacy environments and community knowledge systems—often positioning these as deficient or problematic rather than as assets to build upon. Such approaches directly contradict the community and cultural dimensions of the MELLE framework, which recognise families and communities as partners in literacy development rather than sources of risk requiring management. Further, the proliferation of screening tools and early identification systems, whilst often well-intentioned, can reinforce these risk-based constructions by focusing attention on what children cannot do rather than building upon their existing capabilities. When children as young as three are subjected to literacy screenings that fail to account for linguistic diversity or cultural differences in storytelling traditions, the resulting data often reflects assessment bias rather than genuine learning differences. However, once children are identified as 'at risk', they become subject to what Wilkins and Gobby describe as "intense performance management" that can limit rather than expand their literacy opportunities.

This intensification of risk-based governance has particular implications for the representation dimension of the MELLE framework. When children are constructed as deficient subjects requiring remediation, there is often pressure to focus on 'basic skills' at the expense of engaging with diverse, culturally relevant texts. The current censorship movements discussed in Chapter 5 gain additional power within risk-based governance structures, as diverse books become positioned as distractions from the serious business of addressing deficits rather than as essential resources for affirming children's identities and expanding their perspectives. Furthermore, the economic imperatives driving much educational policy intersect with risk-based governance to create particularly constraining environments for schools serving marginalised communities. When schools are evaluated based on their success in managing risk populations, there is strong pressure to adopt standardised approaches that promise measurable improvements rather than the kind of contextually responsive practices underpinning the MELLE. This creates what Chapter 7 identified as tensions between accountability demands and culturally responsive practice, but the risk-based framework reveals these tensions as more than mere policy contradictions—they represent fundamental conflicts between deficit-based and asset-based approaches to education.

Reimagining Evidence-Based Practice: Expanding Definitions and Methodologies

The concept of 'evidence-based practice' has become central to educational policy and discourse, particularly in literacy education. However, narrow interpretations of what constitutes valid evidence have often privileged particular research methodologies, populations and outcomes while marginalising others. Expanding this definition is essential for creating more equitable literacy education.

Indigenous research methodologies and community-based approaches offer important perspectives that are often excluded from conventional evidence frameworks. These approaches recognise that knowledge is culturally situated, communities hold valuable expertise, relationships significantly influence literacy development, and multiple ways of knowing exist across cultural traditions (Cumming-Potvin et al., 2022; Jackson-Barrett

& Lee-Hammond, 2019; Sisson et al., 2024). Rigney's (2001) foundational argument that Indigenous research methodologies challenge dominant Western paradigms by repositioning Indigenous peoples from objects of research to partners in knowledge creation continues to influence contemporary research approaches. Building on this work, Tuhiwai Smith's (2012) influential decolonising framework demonstrates how recovering Indigenous ways of knowing that have been systematically marginalised by Western academic traditions creates more authentic research partnerships. These enduring contributions to methodological thinking illustrate that incorporating Indigenous perspectives means not abandoning scientific rigor but rather enriching our understanding of what constitutes valid knowledge and meaningful evidence, a principle increasingly embraced in current research practice (Cumming-Potvin et al., 2022; Sisson et al., 2024).

The exemplar presented in Chapter 8 illustrates how supportive policy environments can enable transformative literacy practices. Mikayla's culturally responsive approach to teaching Indigenous knowledge through fish traps exemplifies what becomes possible when educators are given the professional autonomy and resources to implement culturally responsive pedagogies. Her practice demonstrates the importance of policy frameworks that value Indigenous knowledge systems and allow for contextually responsive teaching. However, such practices often exist despite rather than because of current policy environments. The exemplar highlights the need for policies that explicitly value cultural knowledge as evidence, provide time and resources for deep engagement with culturally relevant texts and recognise diverse forms of literacy beyond standardised measures.

In addition to traditional research evidence, the knowledge developed by educators through reflective practice offers important insights for equitable literacy education. This 'practice-based evidence' includes detailed understanding of specific communities, documented successful adaptations of instructional approaches, and knowledge generated through collaborative inquiry. While Cochran-Smith and Lytle (2009) established the foundational concept of "inquiry as stance" in teaching, recent research continues to affirm and extend this approach. Mockler (2020) examines how teachers maintain professional learning and knowledge generation even within highly regulated educational contexts. Similarly, Banegas and Consoli (2021) demonstrate how action research in education creates contextually relevant knowledge that bridges theory and practice in ways traditional research often cannot. This evolving body of work positions teachers as knowledge producers rather than mere implementers of externally developed methods, a principle increasingly recognised as essential for developing responsive literacy practices (Comber & Woods, 2018).

Expanding evidence-based practice also requires broadening the conception of what counts as successful literacy development. Beyond standardised test scores, meaningful measures might include children's engagement and motivation, critical literacy skills, multilingual and multimodal competencies, connection to cultural knowledge and community impact. As discussed in Chapter 7, Dobrescu et al.'s (2022) research on contextual assessment has profound implications for assessment policy and practice. Their study, which involved making simple changes to NAPLAN test papers by replacing unfamiliar terms with locally relevant language, demonstrated "an economically large and statistically significant impact of contextualized test on reading test scores" (Dobrescu et al., 2022, p. 20). The findings that these contextual adaptations could "close the Indigenous reading gap by 50% and reduce the urban rural gap by a third" (Baker, 2021) challenge the very foundations of standardised assessment systems.

An expanded definition of evidence-based practice and assessment does not reject scientific research but rather enriches it by incorporating multiple perspectives, methodologies and measures of success. This expanded view creates space for approaches to literacy instruction that are both rigorous and responsive to diversity.

Principles for Policy Reform: Implementing the MELLE

The evidence and analysis presented throughout this book suggest several principles that should guide policy reform aimed at creating more equitable literacy environments. These principles draw on the core dimensions of the MELLE—quality instruction, opportunity and representation—while recognising the complexity of policy implementation across diverse contexts.

Principle 1: Expand Access to Diverse Reading Materials

Equitable literacy policy must prioritise access to books for all children, particularly those from disadvantaged backgrounds. As Chapter 4 demonstrated, opportunity to read is not merely supplementary but fundamental to literacy development.

Policy initiatives should include:

- Sustained funding for book-gifting programmes beginning from birth
- Technology-enhanced approaches to family literacy support that reach across socioeconomic backgrounds

- Requirements for well-resourced school libraries with qualified librarians and requirements for provision of diverse books
- Targeted support for schools serving disadvantaged communities to build diverse classroom collections

These approaches address the opportunity dimension of the MELLE while recognising that implementation must be responsive to local contexts and needs.

Principle 2: Integrate Cultural Responsiveness Across Educational Systems

Rather than positioning cultural responsiveness as separate from, or opposed to, evidence-based practice, policy frameworks should integrate these approaches at all levels. As the MELLE illustrates, quality instruction that fails to incorporate cultural responsiveness will not serve all children equitably.

This integration requires:

- Embedding cultural responsiveness throughout teacher professional standards rather than as a separate competency
- Requiring knowledge of diverse children's literature and culturally responsive pedagogy in teacher education programmes
- Developing assessment approaches that recognise and value diverse ways of demonstrating literacy competence
- Creating policy frameworks that explicitly support translanguaging and multilingual approaches to literacy development

Scotland's approach to embedding anti-racist education within professional standards provides a promising model for integrating equity considerations throughout educational systems rather than treating them as separate initiatives.

Principle 3: Develop More Inclusive Definitions of Evidence

Policy frameworks should expand definitions of what constitutes valid evidence to include diverse research methodologies, practitioner knowledge and community perspectives. As argued in this chapter, narrow conceptions of evidence have privileged certain methodologies and perspectives while marginalising others, leading to policies that fail to address the needs of diverse learners.

An expanded approach to evidence would:

- Incorporate multiple research traditions and methodologies
- Value Indigenous research methodologies and community-based approaches
- Recognise practitioner inquiry and classroom-based research as legitimate sources of knowledge
- Consider multiple measures of success beyond standardised test scores
- Incorporate evidence about reading engagement, motivation and critical literacy alongside technical skill development

This principle aligns with the contextual dimensions of the MELLE, recognising that effective literacy education must be responsive to cultural, community and contextual factors that shape children's learning.

Principle 4: Address Structural Inequities in Resource Allocation

Creating equitable literacy environments requires addressing the systemic funding disparities that currently limit opportunities for many children. As Rorris (2023) documents, current funding models in Australia persistently disadvantage public schools serving children from low socioeconomic backgrounds, Indigenous communities and culturally diverse populations.

Policy reform should prioritise:

- Funding models that allocate resources based on need rather than reinforcing existing advantages
- Specific allocations for building diverse book collections in schools serving disadvantaged communities
- Investment in library infrastructure and qualified librarians for all schools
- Support for family literacy initiatives that reach across socioeconomic backgrounds

These approaches recognise that creating equitable literacy environments requires not just pedagogical changes but also structural reforms that address resource disparities.

Principle 5: Challenge Risk-Based Constructions of Children and Communities

For policy frameworks to truly align with principles of diversity and equity aligned with the MELLE they must actively resist the construction of children and communities as risk objects requiring management and instead position them as knowledge-holders and partners in literacy development. This principle draws directly on the governmentality analysis provided by Wilkins and Gobby (2024) and recognises that truly equitable literacy education requires fundamental shifts in how policies conceptualise difference and diversity.

This approach requires:

- **Reframing assessment practices** to recognise and value diverse ways of demonstrating literacy competence rather than positioning difference as deficit
- **Developing strengths-based identification systems** that focus on children's capabilities and cultural resources rather than perceived lacks or risks
- **Creating policy language** that positions families and communities as partners with valuable knowledge rather than as sources of risk requiring intervention
- **Establishing accountability measures** that recognise schools' success in building upon community strengths rather than merely managing risk populations
- **Investing in professional learning** that helps educators recognise and challenge deficit assumptions whilst developing skills in asset-based assessment and instruction

This principle recognises that the language and conceptual frameworks used in policy documents shape how children, families and communities are perceived and treated within educational systems. When policies consistently position certain groups as 'at risk' or deficient, they create self-fulfilling prophecies that limit rather than expand educational opportunities. Conversely, when policies recognise and build upon the cultural wealth and linguistic resources that all children bring to their learning, they create conditions for the kind of transformative literacy education described throughout this book and envisioned in the MELLE.

Conclusion: Towards Policy Frameworks that Support Equitable Literacy Environments

The analysis presented in this chapter illuminates both constraints and possibilities within current literacy education policy landscapes. Examining literacy policies through the theoretical lenses of policy mobilities, enactment and practice architectures reveals how global policy flows are recontextualised across multiple levels, creating tensions between standardisation and cultural responsiveness that significantly impact diverse learners. These tensions manifest in narrow conceptions of evidence-based practice, assessment-driven instructional priorities and resource allocation patterns that frequently reinforce rather than address existing inequities.

Particularly significant is the analysis of how risk-based governance structures create what Wilkins and Gobby (2024) describe as "frameworks of calculation and control" that position children from marginalised backgrounds as deficient subjects requiring management rather than as learners with valuable cultural and linguistic resources. This risk-based rationality operates across all levels of policy implementation—from national frameworks that emphasise standardised approaches, to school-level decisions that prioritise remediation over engagement, to classroom practices that focus on managing perceived deficits rather than building upon children's existing capabilities. The pervasiveness of these deficit constructions reveals why equitable literacy education remains elusive despite decades of policy reform: the fundamental ways in which difference is conceptualised within policy discourse work against the asset-based approaches essential for creating truly inclusive learning environments.

The five principles for policy reform outlined in this chapter work synergistically to counter these risk-based constructions whilst creating conditions for the kind of transformative literacy education described in the MELLE framework. Expanding access to diverse reading materials (Principle 1) challenges the notion that all children benefit from monocultural texts by ensuring all learners encounter rich, engaging literature. Integrating cultural responsiveness across educational systems (Principle 2) positions linguistic and cultural diversity as assets rather than deficits requiring remediation. Developing more inclusive definitions of evidence (Principle 3) creates space for the kinds of community knowledge and practitioner wisdom that risk-based governance typically marginalises. Addressing structural inequities in resource allocation (Principle 4) recognises that creating equitable literacy environments requires material changes rather than merely rhetorical commitments to inclusion. Most fundamentally, challenging risk-based constructions of children and communities (Principle 5) demands that policies actively resist deficit framings and instead position families and communities as knowledge-holders and partners in literacy development.

Despite these constraints, pathways towards greater equity exist both within and beyond current systems. Expanding definitions of evidence-based practice to include diverse research methodologies, cultural knowledge and multiple measures of success creates space for approaches that honour children's linguistic and cultural resources while developing essential literacy skills. This expanded conception acknowledges the complex interplay between cognitive dimensions of reading development and the sociocultural contexts that shape children's literacy experiences and identities. By recognising that equitable literacy education requires attention to quality instruction, opportunity to read and authentic representation, policymakers and educators can develop more integrated approaches that address all three dimensions simultaneously.

However, implementing these principles requires sustained resistance to the intensifying risk-based governance structures that construct difference as deficit and position standardisation as the solution to educational inequity. As the analysis in this chapter demonstrates, these structures operate not merely as technical policy mechanisms but also as powerful discursive frameworks that shape how children, families and communities are perceived and treated within educational systems. Transforming literacy education thus requires not only new instructional approaches or resource allocations but also fundamental shifts in the rationalities that govern educational policy—from frameworks of calculation and control towards what might be termed "frameworks of recognition and reciprocity" that honour the knowledge and capabilities that all children bring to their learning.

The principles underpinning the Model for Equitable Literacy Learning Environments offer guidance for policy reform that addresses these interconnected dimensions whilst actively challenging the deficit assumptions embedded in current governance structures. Rather than prescribing universal implementation strategies, these principles acknowledge the complexity of policy implementation across diverse contexts while providing a framework for creating more inclusive and effective literacy education. This approach recognises both the material conditions that constrain current practice and the empowering possibilities for transformation within and beyond existing systems. The evidence presented throughout this book suggests that creating truly equitable literacy environments requires coordinated action across multiple stakeholders—from policymakers to school leaders to classroom teachers—with each playing distinct, but interconnected roles in transforming both the technical and discursive dimensions of literacy education.

The journey towards equitable reading instruction thus emerges as both a technical and an ethical project, requiring not only pedagogical expertise but also critical consciousness about how educational systems can either perpetuate or challenge broader societal inequities. The risk-based governance structures analysed in this chapter reveal that current policy frameworks often reproduce the very inequities they claim to address by positioning difference as deficit and standardisation as the solution. Moving beyond these constraining frameworks requires what this book has termed "equitable literacy environments"—spaces where quality instruction, opportunity to read and authentic representation work together within contexts that recognise and build upon the cultural wealth and linguistic resources that all children bring to their learning.

By reimagining educational equity as a collaborative endeavour involving diverse stakeholders and multiple knowledge traditions, possibilities can be created for literacy education that serves not merely as a means of developing technical skills but also as a pathway toward a more just and inclusive society. This transformation requires sustained commitment to challenging the deficit assumptions that underpin current governance structures whilst building new frameworks that position all children—regardless of background—as capable learners deserving of rich, engaging and culturally affirming literacy experiences. The stakes of this work extend far beyond individual educational outcomes to encompass the kind of society we seek to create: one that values diversity as strength, recognises knowledge in multiple forms, and ensures that every child has the opportunity to see themselves as both a successful reader and a valued member of our shared democratic community.

References

Baker, J. (2021, December 10). 'What's an avocado?': Localising NAPLAN questions lifts scores. *Sydney Morning Herald*. https://www.smh.com.au/national/nsw/what-s-an-avocado-localising-naplan-questions-lifts-scores-20211209-p59g8b.html

Ball, S. J. (2016). Following policy: Networks, network ethnography and education policy mobilities. *Journal of Education Policy, 31*(5), 549–566. https://doi.org/10.1080/02680939.2015.1122232

Banegas, D. L., & Consoli, S. (2021). Action research in language education. In H. Rose & J. McKinley (Eds.), *The Routledge Handbook of Research Methods in Applied Linguistics* (pp. 176–186). Routledge.

Biesta, G. (2010). Why 'what works' still won't work: From evidence-based education to value-based education. *Studies in Philosophy and Education, 29*, 491–503. https://doi.org/10.1007/s11217-010-9191-x

Bishop, R. S. (1990). Mirrors, windows, and sliding glass doors. *Perspectives, 6*(3), ix–xi.

Braun, A., Maguire, M., & Ball, S. J. (2011). Policy enactments in schools introduction: Towards a toolbox for theory and research. *Discourse: Studies in the Cultural Politics of Education, 32*(4), 581–583. https://doi.org/10.1080/01596306.2011.601554

Bus, A. G., Shang, Y., & Roskos, K. (2024). Building a stronger case for independent reading at school. *AERA Open, 10*, 1–17. https://doi.org/10.1177/23328584241267843

Cartwright, N. (2007). Are RCTs the gold standard? *BioSocieties, 2*, 11–20. https://doi.org/10.1017/S1745855207005029

Cochran-Smith, M., & Lytle, S. L. (2009). *Inquiry as Stance: Practitioner Research for the Next Generation*. Teachers College Press.

Coldwell, M., & Moore, N. (2024). Learning from failure: A context-informed perspective on RCTs. *British Educational Research Journal, 50*(3), 1043–1063. https://doi.org/10.1002/berj.3960

Comber, B., & Woods, A. (2018). Pedagogies of belonging in literacy classrooms and beyond: What's holding us back? In C. Halse (Ed.), *Interrogating Belonging for Young People in Schools* (pp. 263–281). Palgrave Macmillan. https://doi.org/10.1007/978-3-319-75217-4_13

Comstock, M., Litke, E., Hill, K. L., & Desimone, L. M. (2023). A culturally responsive disposition: How professional learning and teachers' beliefs about and self-efficacy for culturally responsive teaching relate to instruction. *AERA Open, 9*, 1–18. https://doi.org/10.1177/23328584221140092

Connolly, P. (2017). *Using Randomised Controlled Trials in Education*. SAGE Publications.

Cremin, T., & Scholes, L. (2024). Reading for pleasure: Scrutinising the evidence base: Benefits, tensions and recommendations. *Language and Education, 38*(4), 537–559. https://doi.org/10.1080/09500782.2024.2324948

Cumming-Potvin, W., Jackson-Barrett, L., & Potvin, D. (2022). Aboriginal perspectives matter: Yarning and reflecting about teaching literacies with multimodal Aboriginal texts. *Issues in Educational Research, 32*(4), 1342–1363.

Cushing, I. (2021). 'Say it like the Queen': The standard language ideology and language policy making in English primary schools. *Language, Culture and Curriculum, 34*(3), 321–336. https://doi.org/10.1080/07908318.2020.1840578

Cushing, I. (2023). Policy mechanisms of the standard language ideology in England's education system. *Journal of Language, Identity & Education, 22*(3), 279–293. https://doi.org/10.1080/15348458.2021.1877542

Dobrescu, I., Holden, R. J., Motta, A., Piccoli, A., Roberts, P., & Walker, S. (2022). Cultural context in standardized tests. *UNSW Economics Working Paper*, 2021-08. https://doi.org/10.2139/ssrn.3983663

Ellis, S., & Moss, G. (2014). Ethics, education policy and research: The phonics question reconsidered. *British Educational Research Journal, 40*(2), 241–260. https://doi.org/10.1002/berj.3039

Flores, R., & Rosa, J. (2015). Undoing appropriateness: Raciolinguistic ideologies and language diversity in education. *Harvard Educational Review, 85*(2), 149–171. https://doi.org/10.17763/0017-8055.85.2.149

Gonski, D., Arcus, T., Boston, K., Gould, V., Johnson, W., O'Brien, L., Perry, L.-A., & Roberts, M. (2018). Through growth to achievement: Report of the Review to Achieve Educational Excellence in Australian Schools. Commonwealth of Australia.

Gorur, R. (2016). Seeing like PISA: A cautionary tale about the performativity of international assessments. *European Educational Research Journal*, *15*(5), 598–616. https://doi.org/10.1177/1474904116658299

Hardy, I. (2015). Data, numbers and accountability: The complexity, nature and effects of data use in schools. *British Journal of Educational Studies*, *63*(4), 467–486. https://doi.org/10.1080/00071005.2015.1066489

Jackson-Barrett, E. M., & Lee-Hammond, L. (2019). From Pink Floyd to Pink Hill: Transforming education from the bricks in the wall to the connections of country in remote Aboriginal education. *Australian Journal of Teacher Education*, *44*(10), 35–51. https://doi.org10.14221/ajte.2019v44n10.3

Keddie, A., MacDonald, K., Blackmore, J., Wilkinson, J., Niesche, R., Eacott, S., & Gobby, B. (2020). The constitution of school autonomy in Australian public education: Areas of paradox for social justice. *International Journal of Leadership in Education*, *25*(1), 106–223. https://doi.org/10.1080/13603124.2020.1781934

Lingard, B. (2010). Policy borrowing, policy learning: Testing times in Australian schooling. *Critical Studies in Education*, *51*(2), 129–147. https://doi.org/10.1080/17508481003731026

Lubeck, S., & Garrett, P. (1990). The social construction of the "at-risk" child. *British Journal of Sociology of Education*, *11*(3), 327–340.

MacDonald, K., Keddie, A., Blackmore, J., Mahoney, C., Wilkinson, J., Gobby, B., Niesche, R., & Eacott, S. (2021). School autonomy, school accountability and social justice: A policy overview of Australian public education (1970s to present). *Australian Educational Researcher*, *50*, 307–327. https://doi.org/10.1007/s13384-021-00482-4

Mockler, N. (2020). Teacher professional learning under audit: Reconfiguring practice in an age of standards. *Professional Development in Education*, *48*(1), 166–180. https://doi.org/10.1080/19415257.2020.1720779

National Inquiry into the Teaching of Literacy. (2005). *Teaching Reading: Report and Recommendations*. Australian Government Department of Education, Science and Training.

National Reading Panel. (2000). *Teaching Children to Read: An Evidence-Based Assessment of the Scientific Research Literature and Its Implications for Reading Instruction*. National Institute of Child Health and Human Development.

Parra, J. D., & Edwards, D. B. (2024). Challenging the gold standard consensus: Randomised controlled trials (RCTs) and their pitfalls in evidence-based education. *Critical Studies in Education*, *65*(5), 513–530. https://doi.org/10.1080/17508487.2024.2314118

Ratner, H. (2019). "Describing children at risk: Experiments with context." *Discourse: Studies in the Cultural Politics of Education*, *40*(1), 16–28. https://doi.org/10.1080/01596306.2018.1549701

Rigney, L. I. (2001). A first perspective of Indigenous Australian participation in science: Framing Indigenous research towards Indigenous Australian intellectual sovereignty. *Kaurna Higher Education Journal*, *7*, 1–13.

Rorris, A. (2023). *How School Funding Fails Public Schools: How to Change for the Better*. Australian Education Union.

Rose, J. (2006). *Independent Review of the Teaching of Early Reading: Final Report*. Department for Education and Skills.

Sahlberg, P. (2011). *Finnish Lessons: What Can the World Learn from Educational Change in Finland?* Teachers College Press.

Singh, P., Thomas, S., & Harris, J. (2014). Recontextualising policy discourses: A Bernsteinian perspective on policy interpretation, translation, enactment. *Journal of Education Policy*, *28*(4), 465–480. https://doi.org/10.1080/02680939.2013.770554

Sisson, J. H., Rigney, L. I., Hattam, R., & Morrison, A. (2024). Co-constructed engagement with Australian Aboriginal families in early childhood education. *Teachers and Teaching: Theory and Practice*, *31*(1), 16–30. https://doi.org/10.1080/13540602.2024.2328014

Tuhiwai Smith, L. (2012). *Decolonizing Methodologies: Research and Indigenous Peoples* (2nd ed.). Zed Books.

UNESCO. (2021). *Global Education Monitoring Report 2021/2: Non-State Actors in Education—Who Chooses? Who Loses?* UNESCO Publishing.

Whitaker, M. C., & Valtierra, K. M. (2018). The dispositions for culturally responsive pedagogy scale. *Journal for Multicultural Education*, *12*(1), 10–24. https://doi.org/10.1108/JME-11-2016-0060

Wilkins, A., & Gobby, B. (2024). Objects and subjects of risk: A governmentality approach to education governance. *Globalisation, Societies and Education*, *22*(5), 915–928. https://doi.org/10.1080/14767724.2022.2114073

Wilkinson, J., MacDonald, K., Keddie, A., Gobby, B., Eacott, S., Niesche, R., & Blackmore, J. (2024). School transformation in minoritized settings: A practice architectures lens. *International Journal of Leadership in Education*, 1–19. https://doi.org/10.1080/13603124.2024.2342296

Wright, T. S., Cabell, S. Q., Duke, N. K., & Souto-Manning, M. (2022). *Literacy Learning for Infants, Toddlers, & Preschoolers: Key Practices for Educators*. National Association for the Education of Young Children.

Conclusion

10

Towards a New Paradigm in Reading Education

Reflecting on the Journey: A Synthesis of Key Insights

Throughout this book, I have argued for a fundamental reconsideration of how literacy education, especially reading, is conceptualised and implemented. Three critical insights have emerged from this exploration, each with significant implications for how the teaching of reading is approached in increasingly diverse educational contexts.

First, narrow conceptions of reading instruction that focus exclusively on code-breaking skills while neglecting cultural and contextual dimensions frequently fail to serve all children equitably. As explored in Chapter 3, even the most rigorously designed instructional approaches may falter when they do not account for linguistic and cultural diversity. This does not mean abandoning evidence-based practices but rather expanding our understanding of what constitutes 'evidence' and how these practices can be implemented in culturally responsive ways. The MELLE, introduced in Chapter 2 and expanded in Chapter 7, presents a more comprehensive model that integrates quality instruction with attention to opportunity and representation. This model is built on the understanding that effective literacy education must address not only the technical aspects of reading but also the social, cultural and affective dimensions that influence children's engagement and sense of belonging in literacy learning environments.

Second, persistent opportunity disparities limit many children's access to books and meaningful reading experiences. Chapter 4 documented how inequitable distribution of resources—including books, libraries and time for reading—disproportionately affects children from economically disadvantaged backgrounds and culturally marginalised communities. Despite robust evidence of the benefits of early and sustained exposure to books, many children still lack access to diverse, high-quality reading materials both in school and at home. My Churchill Fellowship investigations revealed that this opportunity disparity exists across many English-speaking countries, with concerning patterns of underfunded school libraries, limited time for independent reading, and barriers to accessing diverse books. These structural inequities contribute significantly to disparities in literacy outcomes, yet they often receive less attention in educational policy than instructional approaches.

Third, authentic representation in children's literature profoundly impacts literacy development. Chapter 5 presented compelling evidence that diverse representation in reading materials positively influences children's engagement, motivation and educational outcomes. When children see themselves and their communities reflected in the books they read, they develop stronger connections to literacy and more positive academic identities. Despite growing awareness of the importance of diverse representation, Chapter 5 documented the persistent lack of diversity in children's books, particularly in educational settings. This representation gap compounds the opportunity disparity, creating additional barriers for children from underrepresented groups. Chapter 6 extended this analysis by examining how children's literature can be used to actively challenge prejudice and discrimination, offering a powerful tool for creating more inclusive and equitable learning environments.

The vignettes of practice presented in Chapter 7 and the exemplar of culturally responsive literacy in action presented in Chapter 8 demonstrated these principles in practice, illustrating how quality instruction, opportunity and representation can be integrated within responsive cultural and community contexts. The exemplar in Chapter 8 provided concrete evidence of the transformative impact of the MELLE when implemented with thoughtfulness and cultural sensitivity. Finally, Chapter 9 examined the policy contexts that shape literacy education, identifying both constraints and possibilities for systemic change. The insights from this exploration reveal the complex interplay between educational policies, institutional practices and classroom implementation, highlighting the need for coordinated action across multiple levels to create more equitable literacy learning environments.

Collectively, these insights challenge conventional assumptions about literacy education and point towards the development of more nuanced, responsive approaches that serve all children equitably. The evidence suggests that creating truly inclusive literacy environments requires attention not just to instructional methods but also to the broader ecological systems that shape children's literacy development and educational experiences.

Reimagining the Reader: Equity, Inclusivity and Opportunity

Central to the MELLE is a reimagining of what it means to be a reader in the 21st century. Traditional conceptions of reading development have often focused narrowly on the acquisition of discrete skills, with success measured primarily through standardised assessments of decoding and comprehension. While these skills are undoubtedly important, they represent only part of what it means to be a flourishing reader in today's diverse and rapidly changing world. The MELLE prompts a reconsideration of what constitutes a successful reader, suggesting a vision that includes not only technical proficiency but also engagement, motivation, critical awareness and cultural competence. Fundamental to this is understanding that children develop as readers within specific social, cultural and historical contexts that shape their opportunities, identities and relationships with texts.

This expanded vision challenges deficit perspectives that have often characterised discussions of literacy development, particularly regarding children from marginalised communities. Rather than viewing linguistic and cultural diversity as obstacles to be overcome, within the MELLE, these diverse attributes are framed as valuable resources that can enhance literacy learning for all children. For example, the children in the exemplar presented in Chapter 8 developed sophisticated literacy skills through an inquiry into Indigenous fishing practices that built upon their cultural knowledge and community connections. This approach honoured the children's existing strengths while expanding their literacy capabilities in meaningful contexts. Similarly, the reluctant reader in Chapter 7 who became "animated" during culturally responsive read-alouds demonstrates how approaches that connect to children's identities and interests can transform their relationship with reading.

Creating equitable literacy environments means ensuring that all children can develop as readers in ways that affirm their identities, build on their strengths, and address their specific needs. It requires moving beyond 'one-size-fits-all' approaches to literacy instruction and assessment to create more responsive and inclusive practices. The MELLE serves as a structure for this reimagining, presenting a way to integrate quality instruction, opportunity and representation within supportive cultural, community, curricular and pedagogical contexts. By attending to all these dimensions, educators can create literacy learning environments where all children have the chance to flourish as readers.

Call to Action: Policy, Practice and the Future of Reading Education

The insights and framework presented in this book point towards a vision of reading education that is both academically rigorous and socially just. Realising this vision requires coordinated action from multiple stakeholders, each with unique responsibilities for advancing equitable literacy education.

For **policymakers**, this vision calls for developing inclusive frameworks that explicitly value diversity and provide resources to support equitable access to books and reading opportunities. Specific policy actions include funding book-gifting programmes like Dolly Parton's Imagination Library, establishing national standards for school libraries, creating incentives for diverse publishing, and ensuring that curriculum and assessment frameworks are culturally responsive. The Scottish example of embedding cultural responsiveness in professional standards for teachers and providing systematic support for anti-racist education offers a promising model for policy development. Similar approaches could be adapted for other national contexts, with appropriate attention to local historical, cultural and political specificities.

For **school leaders**, the MELLE offers a structure for examining current practices and identifying opportunities for greater equity. This might involve conducting audits of classroom and library collections to assess diversity and representation, allocating resources to expand and diversify book collections, providing professional learning focused on culturally responsive literacy instruction, and creating time in the school day for independent reading. School leaders play a crucial role in creating cultures that value diversity and inclusion, setting expectations for culturally responsive practice, and allocating resources to support equitable literacy education. By positioning equity as central to the school's mission rather than as an add-on or special initiative, leaders can create conditions where all children can thrive as readers.

For **educators**, the MELLE provides a practical model for creating more inclusive and effective literacy learning environments. This includes selecting diverse texts that provide both mirrors and windows for all students, implementing instructional approaches that build on children's cultural and linguistic resources, creating meaningful opportunities for engagement with books, and developing assessment approaches that capture the multifaceted nature of literacy development. The exemplars and case studies presented throughout this book offer concrete examples of how these principles can be enacted in diverse educational contexts. They demonstrate that culturally responsive literacy instruction is not an alternative to evidence-based practice but rather an approach that integrates technical expertise with cultural responsiveness to create more effective learning experiences for all children.

For **publishers and authors**, the insights from this book highlight the urgent need for more diverse representation in children's literature and educational materials. The persistent lack of diversity in published books, as documented in Chapter 5, represents a significant barrier to creating inclusive literacy environments. Increasing both the quantity and quality of diverse books—across genres, formats and stage of reading development—is essential for ensuring all children have access to texts that reflect their lives and expand their horizons.

For **families and communities**, the MELLE affirms the valuable role they play in supporting children's literacy development. By recognising and valuing the literacy practices that exist in diverse homes and communities, educational institutions can build more effective partnerships that support children's reading development. Programmes like the Books in Homes and the Indigenous Literacy Foundation demonstrate the power of community-based approaches to expanding access to books and reading opportunities.

For **researchers**, this book identifies numerous areas where further investigation could enhance understanding of equitable literacy education. These include the interplay between instructional approaches and cultural contexts, the long-term impacts of diverse representation on children's literacy development, effective approaches to professional learning for culturally responsive pedagogy and the systems-level changes needed to create more equitable literacy education.

For **teacher educators**, the MELLE offers a structure for preparing future teachers to create equitable literacy environments. As recommended in Chapter 9, initial teacher education programmes should prioritise culturally responsive pedagogy and provide opportunities for preservice teachers to develop the knowledge, skills and dispositions needed for equitable literacy instruction. The exemplar in Chapter 8 demonstrates the transformative impact a teacher with culturally responsive preparation can have on students' literacy learning and cultural identity development.

Collectively, these stakeholders can transform reading education from a site of persistent inequity to a powerful force for creating a more just and inclusive society. By working together across traditional boundaries, they can create literacy learning environments where all children can develop as engaged, critical, and proficient readers.

The Imperative for Transformation

The evidence presented throughout this book makes a compelling case for transforming literacy education to create more equitable outcomes for all children. The persistent disparities in literacy achievement between different groups of students are not inevitable but rather the result of systemic inequities in access to resources, opportunities and culturally responsive instruction. Addressing these inequities is not just an educational imperative but also a moral one, with profound implications for children's life opportunities and for the broader society.

The MELLE offers a useful model to assist this transformation, integrating quality instruction, opportunity and representation within supportive cultural, community, curricular and pedagogical contexts. This integrated approach recognises that effective literacy education cannot be reduced to any single dimension but must address the complex interplay of factors that shape children's literacy development. Creating truly equitable literacy environments requires both technical expertise in literacy instruction and critical consciousness about how educational systems can either perpetuate or challenge broader societal inequities. It demands a commitment to viewing all children as capable learners with valuable cultural and linguistic resources, regardless of their backgrounds or circumstances.

The journey towards more equitable literacy education will not be simple or straightforward. It will require navigating complex political landscapes, challenging entrenched assumptions and developing new approaches to longstanding challenges. As the policy analysis in Chapter 9 revealed, powerful forces continue to push towards standardisation and narrowed conceptions of literacy that may disadvantage children from marginalised communities. However, the examples and evidence presented throughout this book demonstrate that transformation is possible. From the teacher who used culturally relevant texts to help a Sikh student find his voice to the pre-service teacher who created space for Aboriginal students to share their cultural knowledge, these stories illustrate the profound impact of equitable literacy practices on children's educational experiences and outcomes.

The challenge ahead for educators, researchers and policymakers is to develop approaches to reading instruction that honour both the scientific evidence about effective skill development and the sociocultural realities of diverse communities. This is not an either/or proposition but a both/and imperative. By implementing evidence-informed instruction that is simultaneously culturally responsive, we can create truly inclusive learning environments where all children can develop not just as decoders of text, but as meaning-makers, critical thinkers and authors of their own literate futures.

Moving forward, the future of reading education requires literacy learning environments where all children can develop as confident, engaged and critical readers. This necessitates collaborative efforts across roles, institutions and communities to transform literacy education from a reproducer of existing inequities into a mechanism for creating a more just and inclusive society. The Model for Equitable Literacy Learning Environments provides a framework for this transformation—not as a rigid prescription but as a guide for thoughtful reflection and action. The integration of quality instruction, opportunity and representation within responsive contexts enables the creation of literacy learning environments where all children can thrive as readers, thinkers and community members in contemporary educational settings.

Appendix
Research Methodology

Developing the Model for Equitable Literacy Learning Environments (MELLE)

Theoretical and Empirical Foundations

The development of the Model for Equitable Literacy Learning Environments (MELLE) emerged from an iterative process combining multiple research traditions and data sources collected over a 12-year period. This methodological approach draws from both systematic research and practice-based evidence, integrating findings from longitudinal qualitative studies, intensive international fieldwork and collaborative inquiry with educators.

Doctoral Research (2012–2019)

The initial foundations for MELLE were established through my doctoral research investigating culturally responsive book-sharing practices in Australian early childhood (Adam, 2019). This included:

- Five consecutive weekdays of full-day (6 hours per day) observations in the kindergarten room of each of four early education and care centres

- Analysis of 2314 books across these diverse educational settings
- Semi-structured interviews with educators
- Document analysis of policy frameworks and curriculum guidelines
- 27 hours of video-recorded observations of book-sharing sessions
- Systematic coding of book representations using Bishop's (1990) Categories of Cultural Diversity

This research revealed significant disparities in book provision and culturally responsive practices across different socioeconomic communities, establishing the empirical basis for the representation and opportunity dimensions of MELLE.

The Churchill Fellowship: International Fieldwork (2023)

The transformative element in developing MELLE came through my Churchill Fellowship (Adam, 2023), which enabled eight weeks of intensive fieldwork in the United States and United Kingdom. This international investigation employed several methodological approaches:

Institutional Visits and Interviews

- Universities and teacher education programmes (9)
- School districts and classrooms (9)
- Libraries and literacy organisations (7)
- Museums and cultural institutions (8)

Methodological Techniques

- Semi-structured interviews with literacy scholars, educators and other education stakeholders
- Observation of classroom practices and professional learning sessions
- Participatory workshops with educators
- Collection of materials demonstrating best practices

The Fellowship specifically addressed gaps in my previous research by:

1. Examining how different national contexts approached equity in literacy education

2. Identifying successful integration of evidence-based practices with culturally responsive approaches
3. Documenting innovative solutions to resource access challenges
4. Understanding policy translation across educational systems

Synthesis and Model Development

Iterative Framework Building

The MELLE framework developed through:

1. **Theoretical Integration**: Synthesising findings with existing frameworks (Critical Race Theory, culturally sustaining pedagogy, cognitive reading science)
2. **Pattern Recognition**: Identifying successful practices across contexts that addressed all three dimensions simultaneously
3. **Validation Through Practice**: Testing preliminary concepts with educators during fellowship visits and subsequent professional learning

Data Analysis Approach

- Thematic analysis of interview transcripts and field notes using NVivo software for interview transcripts and field notes and Braun and Clark's stages of thematic analysis
- Comparative case study analysis across international contexts
- Member checking with participating educators and institutions

Additional Related Studies

The development of the MELLE was further informed by additional significant studies: a study into the book selection preferences of pre-service teachers (Adam et al., 2021); and an analysis of cultural and family diversity in award-listed Australian children's picture-books (Adam et al., 2024; Adam & Urquhart, 2023). These studies provided additional empirical evidence regarding representation in children's literature and strengthened the theoretical foundations of the model. The full methodological details of these studies can be found in the published works or by contacting the author.

Post-Fellowship Development

Following the Churchill Fellowship, the model underwent further refinement through:

Collaborative Inquiry Cycles (2023–2024)

- Working with Australian schools implementing aspects of the framework
- Targeted reflection sessions with teacher researchers
- Documentation of implementation challenges and successes
- Iterative refinement based on practitioner feedback

Research Validation

- Systematic literature review to ensure theoretical alignment
- Peer review through research workshops and conferences
- External validation through research impact assessment

Methodological Strengths and Limitations

Strengths

- Multi-method approach combining qualitative and practice-based evidence
- International perspective providing comparative insights
- Integration of researcher and practitioner knowledges
- Grounded in both theory and lived experience

Limitations

- Primary focus on English-speaking contexts
- Limited quantitative evaluation of effectiveness
- Potential bias towards innovative practices that may not be widely representative

Ethical Considerations

All research components followed institutional ethics protocols, with particular attention to:

- Informed consent from all participants
- Confidentiality and anonymity protections
- Respectful engagement with Indigenous knowledge systems
- Equitable representation of diverse perspectives

Positionality Statement

As a White Australian researcher living on the unceded lands of the Whadjuk Nyungar People, I acknowledge my positioning within systems of privilege. This awareness has been central to developing a framework that interrogates rather than reproduces dominant cultural assumptions in literacy education. The international fellowship provided crucial opportunities to challenge and extend my own perspectives through sustained engagement with scholars and practitioners from diverse backgrounds.

References

Adam, H. (2023). *Churchill Fellowship Report: To Enhance Expertise in Children's Books as Vehicles for Disrupting Prejudice and Discrimination*. https://www.churchilltrust.com.au/fellow/helen-adam-wa-2022/

Adam, H., Hays, A.-M., & Urquhart, Y. (2021). *The Exclusive White World of Preservice Teachers' Book Selection for the Classroom: Influences and Implications for Practice*. Edith Cowan University, Research Online, Perth, Western Australia, Perth, Western Australia. https://ro.ecu.edu.au/ajte/vol46/iss8/4

Adam, H., Murphy, S., Urquhart, Y., & Katira, A. (2024). Where are the diverse families in Australian children's literature? Impacts and consideration for language and literacy in the early years. *Education Sciences*, 14(9), 1006. https://doi.org/10.3390/educsci14091006

Adam, H., & Urquhart, Y. (2023). A cause for hope or an unwitting complicity? The representation of cultural diversity in award-listed children's picturebooks in Australia. *Bookbird: A Journal of International Children's Literature*, 61(2), 48–58.

Adam, H. J. (2019). *Cultural Diversity and Children's Literature: Kindergarten Educators' Practices to Support Principles of Cultural Diversity Through Book Sharing* Edith Cowan University, Edith Cowan University, Research Online, Perth, Western Australia, Perth, Western Australia]. WorldCat.org. https://ro.ecu.edu.au/theses/2245

Index

Pages in *italics* refer to figures, pages in **bold** refer to tables and page followed by n denotes notes.

academic: performance 43, 142; success 1, 12, 49
accessibility 25, 107, 127
accountability measures 136, 139, 148
achievement gaps 27, 41–42, 44, 100, 110
Active View of Reading 23, 70
adaptations 13, 32, 144–145
African American English (AAE) 26–27, 31–33
alienation 15, 92
autonomous model of literacy, the 28
autonomy 58, 136, 144

best practice 20, 34, 54, 79, 123, 127, 163
Better Beginnings 55, 57
biases 8, 27, 44, 72, 81, 86–89, 101, 108–110, 143, 165; personal 109; racial 108, 110
Black, Indigenous, People of Color (BIPOC) 67
books: access to 5, 14, 41; bans 67–68; censorship 141; critical potential of 15; diversity of 67; gifting 54; interaction with 29; provision of 45, 71; quality 15; sharing 49
Boutte, Gloria Swindler xiv, 30, 34, 41, 43, 107

brain development 44
bridging process *24*
Bus, A.G. 53, 95, 136

Cartwright, K.B. 23, *24*, 25, 70, 135
children 30, 57–58; literacy 20, 57, 80, 100, 109, 114, 150, 157, 159–160; marginalised 13; poverty 42–43
Churchill Fellowship 2–5, 16, 42, 47, 50, 66, 108, 139, 141, 156, 163, 165
classroom environment 74, 106, 124
code-breaking 21, 25, 31–32, 34, 36; role 25; skills 155
Cognitive Foundations Framework 22
cognitive science 1–3, 10, 22, 25–27, 30, 34–35; educational practice and 22
Comber, B. 20, 26, 28, 135, 144
community 10, *11*, 13, 15, 46, 69, 92, 99–100, 102–105, 110, 114, 118–122, 125–129, 139, 145, 156–157, 160; benefits 74; democratic 151; factor, the 15; knowledge 112, 142, 149; leaders 3; libraries 56; partnerships 57, 112; perspectives 146; school 74
comprehension 97; text 50
comprehensive approach 17, 36, 81, 99, 111, 114

Compton-Lilly, C. 28, 41, 43
confidence 32, 55, 73, 95, 103, 106, 113, 122, 126, 128, 138
contemporary relevance 124, 127
content *11*; knowledge 27, 29, 128
Cremin, T. 50–51, 58, 95, 98, 136
critical: praxis 16; questioning 72
crowded curriculum 49, 51
Cultivating Genius (Muhammad) 33
cultural: assumptions 28, 88, 166; bias 8; competence 12, 89, 157; contexts 9–10, 14, 21, 23, 50, 57, 87, 95, 99, 102, 104–105, 110, 126–127, 159; differences 72, 74, 110, 142; heritage 115, 124, 128; identity 30, 67, **78**, 115, 119, 125, 128, 159; knowledge 2, 12–13, 23, 31–33, 35, 70, 72–73, 96, 99, 104–105, 108, 112–113, 115, 120, 122–123, 125, 128, 144–145, 149, 157, 160; needs 141; pluralism 12, 88; responsiveness 10, 16, 30, *36*, 108–109, 111, 115, 133–134, 136, 146, 149, 158–159; values 99
culturally and racially marginalised (CARM) 1, 4–5, 20, 28, 41, 44–45, 49, 59, 66, 132, 137
culturally relevant teaching (CRT) 12, 42
culturally responsive pedagogy (CRP) 3, 12, 21, 71–72, 74, 79, 89, 107–109, 118, 126–127, 132, 139, 141, 144, 146, 159
culturally sustaining pedagogy (CSP) 10, 12, *33*, 88, 164
curriculum *93*, 101, 125; frameworks 101, 138, 140; hidden 9; mandated 8; narrowed 136; Western 31
Cushing, I. 29, 134, 138
cycle of disadvantage 43

decoding 21–22, 25–26, 31–33, 70, 94, 133, 157
deficit: frames 21, 28–29; perspectives 13, 30, 41, 132, 157
Dehaene, Stanislas 22
dialogic spaces 72
differences, cultural and linguistic 28
differentiation 29
digital divide, the 51
disadvantaged populations 142
discrimination 3, 5, 29, 68, 74, 81, 86–89, 115, 156
diverse: learners 13, 21, 23, 27, 31, 33, 101, 111, 146, 149; representation 15, 58, 66, 70–72, 75, **77**, 80, 87–88, 92, 106–107, 140, 156, 159; research 10, 146, 149
Diverse Books for All Coalition 42, 56
diversity 4–5, 14–15, 17, 20–21, 27, 29, 32, 34, 67, 71–79, 81, 87, 96, 99–103, 108–109, 113, 120–121, 124, 128, 133–134, 138, 140–142, 145, 147–149, 151, 155–159, 163–164; gender 103; linguistic 4, 21, 27, 32, 96, 99, 138, 142; student 20; texts, of 15, 32, 36, 50, 70, 75–76, 81, 88, 96, 99, 105, 110, 112, 114–115, 123, 136, 140, 158
Dobrescu, I. 27, 100, 145
Dolly Parton's Imagination Library (DPIL) 54–55, 158
dominant: background 15; dominant narratives 15, 79, 101
Duke, N.K. 23, *24*, 25, 49, 70, 96

early literacy 28, 54, 56–57, 59
education: dichotomies 16; equitable 1, 43, 92, 130, 133; stakeholders 9, 163
educational: debt 41–43, 59; discourse 16, 20, 26; leaders 135, 138–140; policies 1, 8, 28, 46, 51, 81, 107, 130–132, 134–135, 139, 141, 143, 148, 150, 156; practice 9, 16, 22, 30, 50
educators, access to 14
effective reading 3, 9–10, 13, 21, 30–31, 33, 36, 71
empathy 15, 69, 72, 88–89, 98, 106
empowerment 9, 14, 23, 31, 72, 105; personal 17
engagement 25, 92, 98; increased 15
English as an Additional Language/Dialect (EAL/D) 20
equitable education 1, 43, 92, 130, 133
equitable literacy education 12, 23, 36, 65, 80–81, 89, 92, 99, 107, 110, 113, 130, 140–141, 143–144, 148–150, 158–160

equitable literacy learning environments 2, 4, 8–10, *11*, 12–17, 21–22, 26, 28, 30, 32, 34, 36, 42, 44, 46, 48, 50, 52, 54, 56, 58, 60, 66, 68, 70, 72, 74, 76, **78**, 80, 86, 88, 92, 94–96, 98–115, 120, 122, 124, 126, 128, 130, 132, 134, 136, 138, 140, 142, 144, 146, 148, 150, 156, 158, 160–162
equitable outcomes 1, 9–10, 160
equity 1–4, 10, 13, 16–17, 36, 68, 72–73, 81, 108–111, 113, 115, 131, 138–139, 146–147, 149, 151, 157–158, 163
evidence-based practice 1–4, 8–10, 13, 50–51, 71, 95, 115, 132, 135, 143, 146, 149, 155, 159; evolution of 21; expanding 145, 149; need for 27; rethinking 26
expectations, linguistic 29
explicit instruction 2, 21, 26, 31, 54, 93, 94

failure 42, 53, 95; historical 42; moral 42; sociopolitical 42
family 1–2, 15, 21, 27, 29, 41–42, 45, 51, 54–55, 57, 59–60, 67, 75, 99–100, 102, 110, 113, 120, 123, 125, 127, 142, 145, 147–150, 159, 164
Ferguson, D. 48
fieldwork 16, 162–163
Flores, N. 28–30, 134
fluency 22, 25, 27, 33–34, *35*, 49, 94–95, 106–107
formal education 28–29, 45
Four Resources Model 21, 23, 25–26, 32, 35, 88
Free Voluntary Reading (FVR) 49
funds of knowledge 15, 29, 41, 68, 105, 127, 132

gender diversity 103
Grieshaber, S. 42

Hasan, R. 29
Heath, S.B. 28, 46
Hempel-Jorgensen, A. 52
hidden curriculum 9
Hoover, W.A. 1, 22–23

identity 4–5, 13–15, 23, 30, 33, 35, 42, 52, 58, 60, 66–70, 73, **78**, 79–80, 86–87, 95–96, 98–99, 103–105, 111, 115, 119, 125–126, 128, 142–143, 150, 156–157, 159; affirmation 15; reading 14
implementation 13, 16–17, 26, 29, 49–50, 57, 73–75, 94, 99–101, 104, 107, 109–114, *125*, 131–132, 134–135, 138, 142, 145–146, 149–150, 156, 165
inclusion 15, 23, 51, 67–68, 75, 79, 86, 96, 100, 108, 115, 131, 138, 149, 158
independent reading (IR) 14, 49, 53, 94–95, 99, 106–107, 112, 136, 156, 158
Independent Silent Reading (ISR) 49
individual competencies 25
inequity 1–4, 9, 12, 33, 36, 41–43, 45, 47–49, 51, 53–55, 57, 59–60, 66, 81, 87, 113, 115, 131, 137, 139–140, 142, 147, 149–150, 156, 159–161; racial 9
institutional: policies 29; practices 156; structures 36, 130
instructional: approaches 10, 14, 16, 25, 32, 134, 144, 150, 155–156, 158–159; contexts 13
integration 10, 16, 31, 33, 36, 53, 57, 70, 73, 76, 88, 94, 101–103, 106, 114, 118, 123, 127, 134, 146, 161, 164–165
intellectual growth 33
intervention 1, 28, 33, 45, 47–48, 56–57, 71, 74, 86–87, 131, 135, 137, 148; early 86; practical 33

Jackson-Barrett, E.M. 30, 69, 143

Kindytxt 57
King, M. 118
Knight, R. 31
knowledge: cultural 12; generation 9, 144; systems 13, 42, 76, 122, 124, 128, 142, 144, 166
Konza, Deslea 22

Ladson-Billings, G. 9, 12, 42, 45, 87
language 13–14, 20, 22, 26–33, *35*, 43, 57, 70, 74, 96, 99–100, 106, 108, 120–121, 124, 127–129, 133, 138, 145, 148; comprehension 24, 70; oral *35*; variation 26; varieties 26–28, 31–33; written 22

learners, diverse 13, 21, 23, 27, 31, 33, 101, 111, 146, 149

learning: children's 147; difficulties 20; needs 27; opportunities 2, 26, 47, 139; read, to 1, 17, 23, 25; sequence 128; word 22

Lee-Hammond, L. 30, 99, 144

librarians, access to 14

libraries 14, 47–58, 60, 68, 71, 73–76, **77**, 99–101, 111–112, 122, 124, 139–141, 146–147, 156, 158, 163

lifelong learning 1

linguistic diversity 4, 21, 27, 32, 96, 99, 138, 142; expectations 29; resources 2, 13, 29, 33, 96, 142, 148–149, 151, 158, 160

Lipman, P. 46

literacy 1–5, 8–10, 12–17, 20–23, 25–36, 41–60, 65–68, 70–74, 76, **78**, 79–81, 86–89, 92, 94–96, 98–115, 118–151, 155–163, 166; acquisition 20, 31, 46; critical perspectives 8, 25; development 1, 15, 23, 25–26, 30–32, 34–35, 48–49, 51, 57, 66, 70, 80, 96, 99–100, 105, 110–111, 114–115, 132–138, 142–143, 145–146, 148–149, 156–157, 159–160; early 28, 54, 56–57, 59; education 3–4, 9–10, 12, 16, 23, 28–30, 33, 36, 42, 50–53, 65, 74, 80–81, 86–87, 89, 92, 94, 99, 104, 107, 110, 113–115, 118, 123, 127, 130–133, 138, 140–141, 143–144, 147–151, 155–156, 158–161, 163, 166; environments 2, 5, 9–10, 16–17, 23, 34, 42, 54, 57, 60, 65–66, 79–81, 86, 107, 109–111, 114, 118, 122, 128, 132, 138, 140, 142, 145, 147–151, 157, 159–160; gap 29; identities 96; importance 47; instruction 3–4, 8, 16, 23, 30, 33–34, 46–47, 51, 72, 79, 89, 92, 96, 101, 105, 109–110, 112–113, 118–119, 125, 128, 134, 138, 145, 157–160; opportunities 60, 99, 143; pedagogy 8, 51; practices 2, 8, 14, 16, 25, 28–29, 41–43, 46, 59, 72, 86–87, 89, 95, 100–102, 109–110, 123, 140, 144, 159–160; screenings 142; skills 27, 30–32, 36, 54, 73, 88, 92, 127, 145, 150, 157; technical 28, 36

lived experiences 3, 65, 67, 70, 73, 89, 108, 115

mandated curriculum 8

marginalisation 5n1; children 13, 28, 49; communities 3, 14–15, 36, 42–43, 59, 128, 139, 143, 156–157, 160; learners 8; students 15, 29–30, 79, 104

Matthew Effect, the 46

meaning 21, 25, 27, 33–34, 36, 96, 123, 133, 161

mental health 43–44, 68, 87

Merke, S. 53, 95

metacognitive awareness 123

migrant 5

mirrors and windows framework, the 108, 111, 158

misbehaviour 29

Model for Equitable Literacy Learning Environments (MELLE) 4, 8–10, 12–14, 16, 21, 23, 25, 34–36, 58–59, 65, 70, 74, 79–81, 86, 88–89, 92, 94–96, 99–105, 107–115, 118–119, 122, 126, 128, 130, 132, 134, 136–137, 140–143, 145–150, 155–164

moral: commitment 17; failure 42

motivation 14, 23, 49, 52, 55, 65–66, 69–70, 95, 97, 98, 106–107, 111, 126, 142, 145, 147, 156–157

Muhammad, G. 30, 33, 102

multilingual awareness 32

narratives 15, 20, 29, 44, 75, 79, 99, 101, 106, 113, 123, 141; deficit-based 20

National Assessment of Progress in Literacy and Numeracy (NAPLAN) 27, 44, 55, 100, 134, 145

On Country Learning (Jackson-Barrett and Lee-Hammond) 30

opportunity *11*, 25, *59*, 92, 96, *97*; inequity 43, 56; read, to 14, 17; representation and 96, *97*

oral language 22, 27, *35*, 106

orthographic mapping 22

pattern recognition 164

personal: empowerment 17; transformation 31

phonemic awareness 22, 25–26, 34, 96

phonics: approaches 26; instruction 10, 17, 22, 27, 31, *35*, 94–96, 106–107, 132

phonological awareness 22, *35*, 106, 133

policies: enactment 131–132; implications 137; institutional 29; mobilities 131, 148; reform 113, 145, 147, 149–150; surveillance 138
policymakers 3–4, 56, 138, 140, 150, 158, 160
poverty 42–46, 141–142; child 42–43
power 5, 8–9, 14–16, 25, 28, 31, 35, 46, 72, 79, 87–89, 94, 101, 103–104, 112, 115, 143, 159; structures 9, 14, 16, 28, 88, 101
practices, institutional 156
prejudices 3, 5, 15, 68, 81, 86–89, 92, 104, 156; harmful 15
privilege 1, 9, 15, 28, 36, 79, 88–89, 132–135, 138, 143, 146, 166
professional: development 50, 56, 74, 89, 109–110, 112, 114, 139; learning 73–74, 108, 110, 112–113, 134, 136, 139, 144, 148, 158–159, 163–164
Proudest Blue, The (Muhammad and Ali) 102
psychological factors 23, 70

quality instruction 3–4, 10, *11*, 13–14, 17, 20–21, 23, 25, 27, 29, 31, 33–36, 58–59, 65–66, 79–81, 88–89, 92, *93*, 94–96, 98–103, 105, 107–108, 111–112, 114–115, 118–119, 122, 126, 128, 130, 134, 137, 140, 145–146, 150–151, 155–157, 160–161

racial inequities 9
raciolinguistic ideologies 29, 133
racism 34, 44, 74, 87, 89, 115
reading 20; cognitive processes underlying 22; comprehension 22, 27, 49; development 8, 21–23, 25, 31, 35, 48, 70, 150, 157, 159; development theory 21; difficulties 27; effective 21; engagement 51–52, 60, 107, 111, 114, 133, 147; fluency 49, 106; identities 14, 52, 111; instruction 1–4, 9–10, 13, 20–22, 25–31, 33, 36, 45–46, 52–53, 60, 65, 74, 107, 130, 132, 138–140, 150, 155, 160; learning to 1, 17, 23, 25; pleasure, for (RFP) 14, 44, 49–54, 56, 58, 98, 136; role 23; opportunities 14, 17, 47; proficiency 1, 10, 53, 95, 110, 138;

programmes 14; skilled 22; social practice, as a 21–22; shared 106–107, 112; success 30, 70; teaching 25
Reading Rope, Scarborough's 22
reflective practice 105, 110, 144
reform 1, 71, 113, 132–133, 135, 145, 147, 149–150
regulation: emotional 43; self 23, *24*
representation *11*, 14–15, 25, 66–67, 76, **77**, *80*, 92, *93*, 107, 124, 126, 140; cultural 76; diverse 15, 58, 66, 70–72, 75, **77**, 80, 87–88, 92, 106–107, 140, 156, 159; opportunity and 96, *97*
research, diverse 10, 146, 149
resource allocation 43, 111, 113–114, 130, 133, 136–137, 139, 147, 149–150; inequitable 156
responsive practice 2–3, 94–95, 108–109, 134–135, 143, 158, 163
revolutionary love 30
roles 9, 21, 23, 25, 32, 60, 70, 104–105, 138, 150, 161; society, in 9
Rosa, J. 28–29, 134

scaffolded learning 119–122, 125, 127
science of reading 10, 21, 23, 26
Seidenberg, M.S. 1, 8, 20–23, 26, 28, 31–33
self-regulation *24*
shared reading 106–107, 112
Simple View of Reading, the 22–23
skill acquisition 86, 95
Snell, J. 29
social: cohesion 87, 89; justice 2–3, 8, 10, 15–16, 43, 57–58, 72, 88–89, 98, 108, 130, 136, 139; practice, reading as a 21–22; transformation 9, 12, 17, 31, 86, 89
societal transformation 31
socioeconomic: backgrounds 14, 20, 57, 60, 89, 142, 145, 147; conditions 44, 47; dimension 47; disadvantage 46; disparities 43; diversity 100; factors 2, 46; inequities 60; levels 52; mobility 1; reality 45; status 4, 28–29, 42, 44, 51; strata 57
sociopolitical: consciousness 12; contexts 8; environment 16; failure 42; educational needs 20
Souto-Manning, Mariana xiv

stakeholders 9, 56, 60, 131, 133, 138, 150–151, 158–159, 163
standardisation 21, 29, 132–134, 136, 139, 149–150, 160
stereotypes 15, 72, 75, **77**, 79, 87, 89, 98, 103; harmful 15
storytelling 42, 99, 105, 142
Street, B. 28, 46
structures, institutional 36, 130
student: agency 104, 123; reading choices 15
successful reader 20, 151, 157
Swartz, M. 56
systematic phonics instruction 14, 22, 35, 106–107
systems of power 8

teachers 32–33
Teaching English to Speakers of Other Languages (TESOL) 27
teaching reading 25, 46, 103
text: analysis 21; analyst 21, 23, 25, 70, 88, 101; comprehension 50; diversity of 15, 32, 36, 50, 70, 75–76, 81, 88, 96, 99, 105, 110, 112, 114–115, 123, 136, 140, 158; participant 21, 25, 32, 70; user 21, 25, 32, 70
theoretical integration 164
traditions 10, 21, 25, 27, 33, 42, 99, 124, 142–144, 147, 151, 162
transformation: personal 31; societal 31
Tunmer, W.E. 1, 22–23

underrepresented groups 69–70, 98, 156

validation 164–165
virtuous cycles 70
vocabulary 10, 22, 25, 34, *35*, 49–50, 70, 94, 106–107, 121, 125

Washington, J.A. 20, 26, 28, 31–33
Ways with Words (Heath) 46
Williams, G. 29
Woods, A. 20, 26, 135, 144
word: learning 22; recognition *35*, 70
written language 22

For Product Safety Concerns and Information please contact our EU
representative GPSR@taylorandfrancis.com
Taylor & Francis Verlag GmbH, Kaufingerstraße 24, 80331 München, Germany

www.ingramcontent.com/pod-product-compliance
Lightning Source LLC
Chambersburg PA
CBHW071205240426
43668CB00032B/2100